About the Authors

Cheryl Canfield is an instructor of the Hypnotherapy Training Institute. She has practiced as a Clinical Hypnotherapist and Wellness Counselor since 1993 and has taught at many International Hypnotherapy Conferences.

Cheryl's award-winning book, *Profound Healing,* is an exploration of the steps in her healing process and the insights derived during her inspiring recovery as she journeyed from advanced cancer to radiant health. It is valuable for health and counseling professionals and for those dealing with catastrophic illness for her deep insights on physical, emotional and spiritual healing. This book has received rave reviews from Joseph Chilton Pearce, Wayne Dyer, Caroline Myss and Gerald Jampolsky.

Cheryl is the editor of several major hypnotherapy texts and was managing editor of the monthly newsletters of the American Council of Hypnotist Examiners. She is also co-compiler of *Peace Pilgrim: Her Life and Work in Her Own Words,* a spiritual classic with over 500,000 copies in print and is President of the non-profit organization Friends of Peace Pilgrim.

Randal Churchill is founder, Director and primary instructor of the Hypnotherapy Training Institute, which became one of the first licensed hypnotherapy schools in 1978. Known as "The Teacher of the Teachers,"™ he has trained many of the state-approved hypnotherapy instructors in the United States. HTI draws students from various countries to the San Francisco area each semester and has an alumni of thousands of graduates.

Randal was the first President of the American Council of Hypnotist Examiners and completed several terms over the years. Known for its high standards, this is the original Hypnotherapy Certification organization. A veteran of over 50,000 hours of a hypnotherapy practice spanning 50 years, he received his degree in Psychology with Honors from Sonoma State University.

An intuitive, supportive therapist, Randal is originator of Hypnotic Dreamwork™ and a pioneering leader of regression, Gestalt therapy, and advanced ideomotor methods. *Become the Dream* was the first book about the integration of dreamwork and hypnotherapy. His classic *Regression Hypnotherapy* demonstrates his revolutionary work in overcoming the effects of trauma and has been called the most important text about regression ever published. The companion volume, *Catharsis in Regression Hypnotherapy,* has been published to rave reviews.

Churchill-Canfield's Law

What Can Go Right Will Go Right

Cheryl Canfield

&

Randal Churchill

CHURCHILL-CANFIELD'S LAW: What Can Go Right Will Go Right
is printed on acid free, natural recycled paper.

Transforming Press
email: transformp@aol..com
www.transformingpress.com

ISBN 978-0-9656218-5-4

1. Psychology 2. Self-Help 3. Hypnotherapy

FIRST EDITION. Printed in the United States of America

10 9 8 7 6 5 4 3 2

This book is dedicated to the inspired and wise leaders, poets, sages and healers throughout time, who through steadfast example have demonstrated courage and conviction even in the midst of enormous challenges, and continue to guide humankind toward the amazing potential we all have to become compassionate caretakers of the earth and the generations that will follow us;

To our own families who have supported, learned and grown with us;

And to our graduates, students and clients and all those with whom we are privileged to work and serve.

In these challenging times, as technology advances and the future looks uncertain, it is our hope that more and more of us learn and lead in the ways of peace and compassion for the preservation of our beautiful planet and highest good of all.

Contents

Introduction

Besides its value for personal growth, this book is useful for those in the helping professions, including counselors, therapists, teachers, coaches and medical professionals, to further develop a transformational framework for teaching elevating and positive viewpoints with clientele or students. This book is designed to emphasize reframing to positive perspectives, including the big picture, as this is often such an important aspect of helping clients and students make powerful and lasting change in their lives.

From the beginning we focus on the creative power of the mind as we learn to put our attention on what we want to see happen. Reframing a belief in lack or limitation can open up unlimited potential in our ability to manifest all the good things we would like to see happen. Throughout this book the idea is reinforced over and over that where our attention goes our energy follows. Chapter 5, *Reframing*, specifically addresses the issue of reframing as a valuable tool to recognize and change limiting beliefs and habit patterns that have continued to have a negative effect in one's life.

Our perceptions begin to form early in life and they provide the lenses through which we see. They influence our behavior and our reactions to the outside world as well as how we perceive ourselves. We hope to inspire an expanded recognition that can open us up to new levels of awareness, unleashing the power of the mind as we learn to utilize all of its aspects – the conscious, subconscious and superconscious. By consciously directing – in meditation and hypnosis – how we want to be, we can become the person we choose to be. Every one of us has incredible potential, much more than we customarily realize. We limit ourselves by thinking things can't be done – so we don't even try. If we think something can be done, we might surprise ourselves by how successfully the task is accomplished.

When someone told the American sage, Peace Pilgrim, that something couldn't be done her response was, "I'm so glad I didn't know because I've already done it." Chapter 16, *Peace Pilgrim: The Teachings of a Modern Mystic,* tells the story of a woman who didn't believe in limitations. She understood that by living in accordance with universal laws of peace and harmony everything that could go right would. She took the name Peace Pilgrim and set out during the McCarthy era on a pilgrimage that lasted until her death over 28 years later.

It is our hope that the readers, students, teachers and those in the healing professions who look through these pages will be inspired to test the principles herein and to look inside to the still small voice within, that connection to our own inner teacher, wisdom and compassion. Meditation and hypnosis are powerful doorways to that inner voice. The world around us is calling us to be a part of the stirring and awakening. The planet and our very lives lie in the balance. We can all use our power and influence to turn the prevailing tide toward a golden age of peace, compassion and recognition that we're all cells in the body of humanity, all part of the whole.

Learning to go within and connect with the power of our own inner voice and guidance empowers us to create lives of incredible meaning, purpose and fulfillment. We begin to more fully understand that we are here on purpose – for a purpose – and have the potential to find our unique path and calling. Most of us are aware of having quiet moments when we open up to beautiful inspirations, then often later discount them as we bring them into the realm of the rational mind, the great debater. With strong arguments from both sides we are soon overwhelmed and confused. When we don't act on the inspirations that come they become unrealized potential.

We have put together the content of this book from our collective years of experience in the field of self-transformation, grounded by a powerful foundation in hypnotherapy, both in private practice and as instructors of hypnotherapy. Randal Churchill founded the Hypnotherapy Training Institute (HTI) in 1978 where he continues as director and primary instructor. In this book he shares his passion for teaching hypnotherapy skills to those in the health and healing fields and those looking to expand their awareness to find healing and transformation in their lives. Chapter 36, *Our Relationship to the Earth: The Great Challenge,* addresses his (our) passion for the need to work collectively on the healing and nurturing of our beautiful planet and all life for now and for all future generations.

Cheryl Canfield undertook her studies at HTI more than 25 years ago, after recovering from advanced cancer. Without radical treatment she was told she might not live six months. After experiencing a spontaneous image of herself dead on the operating table, she decided to forego conventional treatment and began researching and implementing a holistic course of personal and spiritual healing meant to prepare her for that final transition. Instead, she experienced a profound inner healing that led to physical healing. She writes about her experience in Chapter 17, *Cheryl's Story: Profound Healing*. She has had a private practice as a Wellness Counselor and Clinical Hypnotherapist for 25 years and has been the other primary instructor with Randal since 2011.

Randal developed the concept, What Can Go Right Will Go Right, when HTI was founded, and referenced it in classes. Cheryl and Randal mentioned it in 1997 in the first edition of the book *Become the Dream*, and got inspired at that time to expand the concept into this book that we've developed over many years. It has been a journey through our life experiences, our passions, our shared perspectives and differences. We have pulled the best and sometimes the hardest of what life has taught us, what we've learned from those who have inspired us – our families, our friends and those we've been honored to teach, counsel and work with. We've shared many of our own stories and continually strive to demonstrate the capacity for healing and growth that is inherent in our human experience. As we act on the inspirations that come we are guided to explore the limitless potential and opportunities we are given to learn and grow. We continue to deepen our understanding and demonstrate, to the best of our ability, the gifts that we are given.

Randal has written many deep and exceptional text books on the extraordinary healing capability of hypnotherapy as he powerfully demonstrates in his books and classes. After completing the advanced and graduate courses of HTI, Cheryl was given the opportunity to further her learning through the ensuing years by editing a succession of Randal's books. Her sensitive and insightful editing brings out the generosity and compassion that resonates throughout his work.

Randal and Cheryl met in 1992 when Cheryl signed up for his classes. Three years earlier, when diagnosed with advanced cancer, she had begun writing a book with the tentative title *Dying Well,* which ultimately changed to *Profound Healing*. As she and Randal developed a friendship he continually encouraged her to bring her book to fruition and publication. He alternately encouraged her writing and the telling of her story, inspiring her to keep moving forward until the book was published in 2003.

We have known each other for over a quarter of a century, working together and separately through many years. Our friendship deepened over the years as we shared a path of service that culminated near the end of this latest endeavor. In the spirit of this book's theme, a transformative moment moved our personal relationship forward and we married during the publication of *Churchill-Canfield's Law: What Can Go Right Will Go Right.* We joined our lives not as a young couple starting out to discover ourselves and the world, but having already discovered the world, what's really important and what has true value. We continue our renewed passion to teach and speak on the tremendous potential we all have to heal and live meaningful lives that support our personal growth and serve the good of the whole.

-Cheryl Canfield and Randal Churchill

Don't be afraid to demand great things of yourself. Powers which you never dreamed you possessed will leap to your assistance. – Orison S. Marden

When you are inspired by some great purpose, some extraordinary project, all your thoughts break their bounds. Your mind transcends limitations, your consciousness expands in every direction, and you will find yourself in a new, great and wonderful world. - Patanjali

Good fortune is what happens when opportunity meets with preparation. - Thomas Edison

Love the moment, and the energy of that moment will spread out beyond all boundaries. – Corita Kent

I learned that it is possible for us to create light, sound and order within us no matter what calamity may befall us in the outer world. – Helen Keller

You could cover the whole world with asphalt, but sooner or later green grass would break through. - Ilya Ehrenburg

Cultivate peace of mind which does not separate one's self from one's surroundings. When that is done successfully, then everything else follows naturally. - Robert M. Prisig

What we achieve inwardly will change outer reality. - Otto Rank

The world is not to be put in order; the world is order, incarnate. It is for us to harmonize with this order. - Henry Miller

There is no security on this earth, only opportunity. - Douglas MacArthur

In the middle of every difficulty lies opportunity. - Albert Einstein

All things are possible until they are proved impossible and even the impossible may only be so, as of now. - Pearl S. Buck

I have become my own version of an optimist. If I can't make it through one door, I'll go through another door - or I'll make a door. Something terrific will come no matter how dark the present. - Rabindranath Tagore

CHAPTER 1

What Can Go Right Will Go Right

Churchill-Canfield's law is the opposite of the concept of Murphy's law. Responding to a setback with the idea that anything that can go wrong will go wrong can be discouraging or funny. It can also set up negative expectations. The mind is powerful and what is focused on tends to manifest. Churchill-Canfield's law is a validation of the power and potential of the mind to move in a positive direction - which is encouraging and more fun –and produces far better possibilities. The very idea of what can go right will go right, may seem provocative considering all the suffering in the world and the challenges we often have in our lives. But when something is considered possible or hopeful, we tend to take action that leads in some constructive direction. If we think something is impossible or have a negative expectancy, chances are we won't even try.

The concept of Murphy's Law can be useful, if not taken literally, to encourage caution and thoroughness to protect against potential problems. But even for that purpose, the healthier and ultimately more effective attitude is to frame the challenge in a positive way, to be inspired to strive for excellence and safety, rather than having a negative fear-based perspective that can easily lead to focusing on the negatives in other aspects of our lives.

In many aspects of our daily lives, what can go right, will go right; whatever can go wrong, will go wrong - whichever you believe, you are likely to be right. Our beliefs have to do with the attitudes we have developed and our attitudes have everything to do with the way we perceive and respond to our experiences. Another way to put it is that an optimist acts on causal consciousness (a participant in events) to take whatever action is necessary for the best outcome. A pessimist falls into non-action through victim consciousness (a perception of non-participation) as a recipient of circumstances.

Sometimes it takes something going wrong to call our attention to all that has gone right. Most of the time we have an incredible abundance in many areas of our lives that we're not even paying attention to or acknowledging. Too often we focus on the negative experiences in our lives while the every day abundance of things going right gets forgotten or isn't even considered. Or we may have a tendency to put all of our attention on the one thing that isn't working while not taking notice of all the things that are working. While it is important to look at the thing that's going wrong for the purpose of doing something about it, we don't want to get stuck in that focus.

Optimists see the parts of their lives that are working well and what they would like to see happen. Pessimists see the parts that are not working well and what negative possibilities could happen. We want to be realistic and make wise decisions in our lives, and we can learn to do that with an optimistic attitude rather than a pessimistic one. Usually most of the things in our lives are working just fine. Our children are alert and healthy, the car starts fine, we have enough food to eat, heat to keep warm, we have good connections with people, and so on. Pessimists focus on something negative or what negative thing might possibly happen. They wake up wondering what is going to go wrong today, fearing that something will. They'll be right.

Even when times are difficult, more good things than bad are usually happening at the same time. For example, the Great Depression of the 1930's brought out the worst and the best in people, depending on where attention was focused. A lot of people took their losses to heart and saw only what was gone. Others looked around and saw that they still had many things that really matter such as a home, family, friends, experience, and an opportunity to start over. Many who grew up during the Depression experienced that people shared more and were less afraid of each other. One woman, for example, remembered that strangers were often welcomed into her home as honored guests. When she and her siblings had birthdays her father would go outside and invite anyone who happened by to come in and join them. Whenever she went to her cousin's house, rich by her family's standards, it was considered a welcome treat to be given an orange. As a family they learned to see and appreciate ordinary things.

When you're thinking in terms of what can go wrong (victim consciousness), you might change lanes while driving and think, "Not again! I change to the faster lane (or checkout line) and it slows down!" There is a miracle going on if you choose to change your focus. In relatively recent human history there were no cars. If you're driving a car that probably means you own a car. Most people in the world don't own a car, and compared to most people and especially by the overwhelming standards of history you're fabulously wealthy.

If the worst thing that happens at the moment is that you change into a lane and it slows down, you're doing pretty well. You probably have gas in the tank and tread on the tires. You didn't just get into an accident or have a heart attack or stroke. You're not getting stopped by a police officer. More good news: If you're bothered because you're driving in a lane that has slowed down more than the other lane, then you're probably not worried about being in a raging blizzard. What a wonderful change of perspective when we wake up to the miraculous world we live in. Are you really on a time schedule at this particular moment or are you in a habit of hurrying? Or maybe you have a job and you're late. Congratulations, you've got a job. And you have a choice. You can get in the habit of leaving earlier and relax.

Universal law affects every level and aspect of reality. These laws are continually working toward balance and harmony. How else do all of the laws of the universe continue for eons? From our perspective, the stars continue to stay in the sky and the days and nights rotate. As human beings, however, we use our minds to work with or against this natural tendency toward harmonious outcomes. Thus we call into play that law of mind: What we focus on we tend to manifest. We learn to balance optimism with realism.

If you recognize the value of being more optimistic but seem to experience the world as if Murphy's law often rules, science can teach us that such instances are a form of *confirmation bias* in which someone (at least subconsciously) seeks out evidence to confirm already formed ideas. Similarly, *selection bias* ensures that those expectations in which Murphy's law seems to occur are remembered and the many times it was not true are forgotten. Murphy's law can also be stated in mathematical terms and disproved using the *principle of least action*.

If you focus on what can go wrong, look for things to go wrong, you will no doubt collect a preponderance of frustrating experiences and be living proof of all the things that aren't working. If, however, you focus on the best possible outcomes, all the things that can go right, and work to do your part, you may awaken to the myriad of miracles that are waiting for you. It may be that a particular outcome won't be what you wanted or expected. Chances are it will be better, even if you don't see that in the beginning.

To check out this hypothesis and see where you stand, recall some of the events in your own life that may not have gone the way you anticipated or wanted at the time. A sweetheart or spouse broke your heart by breaking off the relationship or asking for a divorce and it seemed you might never heal. If you are a pessimist, you may be balking whenever an opportunity comes along to enter a new relationship because you can't trust another person. Probably you don't trust your own judgment either. (If I made the wrong choice before I'll probably do it again.) The world can't be trusted, for that matter, because bad things happen. If you are an optimist you might realize that you learned some valuable lessons, or if it hadn't happened you wouldn't have found the love of your life that came later, or you might not have found your own strength and wholeness outside of a relationship. In the big picture you may now recognize that event as ultimately beneficial. How we perceive the world is often the result of a habit pattern that developed early in life. With awareness, we can choose to develop a positive attitude and perception in life, opening ourselves to wonderful possibility and potential.

I have often thought it would be a blessing if each human being were stricken blind and deaf for a few days during his early adult life. Darkness would make him more appreciative of sight; silence would teach him the joys of sound. - Helen Keller

The world is full of wonders and miracles but man takes his little hand and covers his eyes and sees nothing. - Israel Baal Shem

If I were to begin life again, I should want it as it was. I would only open my eyes a little more. - Jules Renard

Most human beings have an absolute and infinite capacity for taking things for granted. - Aldous Huxley

When it comes to life the critical thing is whether you take things for granted or take them with gratitude. - G.K. Chesterton

We are living in a world of beauty, but few of us open our eyes to see it. - Lorado Taft

The real voyage of discovery consists not in seeking new landscapes but in having new eyes. - Marcel Proust

To think creatively, we must be able to look afresh at what we normally take for granted. - George Kneller

One very important aspect of motivation is the willingness to stop and to look at things that no one else has bothered to look at. This simple process of focusing on things that are normally taken for granted is a powerful source of creativity. - Edward de Bono

When something does not insist on being noticed, when we aren't grabbed by the collar or struck on the skull by a presence or an event, we take for granted the very things that most deserve our gratitude. - Cynthia Ozick

To educate yourself for the feeling of gratitude means to take nothing for granted, but to always seek out and value the kindness that stands behind the action. Nothing that is done for you is a matter of course. - Albert Schweitzer

In all affairs it's a healthy thing now and then to hang a question mark on the things you have long taken for granted. - Bertrand Russell

CHAPTER 2

Taking Things for Granted

"I want a divorce," she says.

"Why in the world do you want a divorce?" he asks in shock.

"Why? I can't even remember the last time we had a real conversation!"

Most things are working with so little effort or thought on our part that we can easily slip into taking them for granted. (Husbands, wives and significant others take note!) Lots of good things can be taking place and we're not even paying attention:

My partner has dinner on the table every night; makes sure the oil in my car has been changed; picks the kids up from school or drives the kids to events. The roses that were planted in spring are still blooming in December. The car hasn't broken down in months. I wake up every morning and there's a gorgeous woman/handsome man next to me, albeit somewhat disheveled. Well, maybe not exactly gorgeous or handsome, but WARM and ALIVE. (And if you're not in a relationship, you could be grateful for the potential, the hope, or for the flexibility and freedom that you currently have.)

All kinds of good things are happening if we stop to think about it. In fact, problems are often solutions to previous problems. We're so frustrated by the socks on the floor or the toilet seat being left up that we forget how lonely we once felt or how much we longed to have that special someone to share our life with.

Looking at technology, today we have the internet and all manner of electronic gadgets which advance so quickly we can hardly keep up. Looking back, we acquired computers, cordless phones, fax and answering machines, then portable computers and cell phones, then smartphones that could go everywhere with us. We went from black and white to color to flat screen televisions. Before that we had no television, no radio, no phones, no telegraph. In the realm of transportation, it's common for many people to use cars, and sometimes jets for longer trips. Just over a hundred years ago we had only horse and buggy, trains and steam ships - faster than the sailboats that were major transportation and transport before that. We've become so accustomed to modern conveniences and advances that we really can't imagine not having them.

Many of us alive today have been born into a world of luxury in which we don't even realize the contrast of a few hundred years ago, or even a few short decades. For example, the convenience of indoor plumbing and warm running water for daily showers or baths. Earlier bathing rituals, for those fortunate enough to have indoor plumbing, meant the family tub was filled with hot water heated over the fire. The man of the house would get the privilege of enjoying the nice clean water. Then all the other sons and men, then the women, and finally the children. Last were the babies. By then the water was pretty thick. Thus, the saying, "Don't throw the baby out with the bath water."

Houses had roofs of thick straw called thatch, that reached nearly to the ground at the sides. There was no supporting wood framework. The nice, thick straw was where little animals liked to go to get warm. All the pets - dogs, cats and other small animals, plus mice, rats and bugs, all lived on the roof. When it rained it became slippery, so sometimes the animals would slip and fall through the roof. Thus the saying, "It's raining cats and dogs."

There was also nothing to prevent things from falling through the roof into the house, so people did their best to keep things clean. This could pose a real problem in the bedroom where bugs and other droppings from animals could land on the bed. Genius is born of necessity - or desperation. Someone discovered that big bed posts could be put up with a sheet hung over the top to protect the bed from unwanted messes. Thus the origin of modern four poster beds and beautiful canopies.

Many houses in earlier times had dirt floors, which explains where the expression "dirt poor" came from. The wealthy often had slate floors, an improvement over dirt, but in winter the floors became slippery when wet. Thresh was spread on the floor during wet seasons to help inhabitants keep their footing. As the winter wore on more and more thresh was added until when the door was opened it would start to slip outside. A piece of wood at the entryway was added to prevent this loss and called a "thresh hold."

Cooking was done over a fire in the kitchen or parlor. A big pot was hung over the fire which would be lit every morning. Into the pot would go whatever edibles were available, mostly vegetables with occasional meat. The resulting stew would be eaten for dinner and leftovers stayed in the pot to get cold overnight. In the morning the fire was lit and the process started all over. Often a portion of the stew would have been in there for days - thus the rhyme, "Peas porridge hot, peas porridge cold, peas porridge in the pot nine days old."

Conditions at the time that the United States was being founded were vastly different from current times. Getting from one state to another was difficult and it might take weeks to travel across several states. Elections were designated for early November because in those early days of our government, it took time to get the news of elections around the country. Many women in those same times were in such poor health that they couldn't produce breast milk and had to chew up meat for their babies. In the late 18th century half of the children in some areas, such as among the Irish in Boston, didn't live past the age of five. In America in 1900 the life expectancy had grown to 47 years. In 2018 it was 79.3 years.

In today's world we can walk down the street and pass by people who are living with the heart, kidney, or liver of a donor. We have people communicating across cultures, speaking two or three or more languages. It may be across vast oceans by internet, or phone line and satellite, or a day's travel by plane. The quality of life has improved dramatically in many countries, especially for women and minorities. Although there is much that still needs to be achieved along these lines, the progress made in just one century boggles the mind. For example, only 66 years after the Wright Brothers accomplished the first successful airplane flight ever, Neil Armstrong took his first step on the moon.

Sometimes it isn't until something happens that we realize how much we have. We don't think about how convenient and exhilarating it is to have legs to walk around on until we break one; or we sprain a wrist and realize how dependent we are upon our hands for the simplest to the most complex task. This point was particularly brought home when I ran into an acquaintance I hadn't seen in awhile. She explained that she'd had an unfortunate fall – during which she caught her weight on her arms and broke them both. I immediately sympathized with her, but it wasn't until she described her utter dependency on her husband for everything (truly everything!) that I fully realized how much I appreciate the functionality of my whole body, and how often I have taken this miracle for granted.

We live in a country and at a time that is particularly prone to taking things for granted because we experience an incredible abundance on the material and technological side of life. It is easy under such circumstances to get lulled into moving through life in a fog or a frenzy – until a cosmic wake-up call comes along. Such messages make us aware of how much we have to be grateful for, and these transforming moments may be joyful or sobering or both. We find ourselves heading for disaster, skidding out of control, and somehow we are saved. We stop short of crashing into the cement divider or going over the cliff. Most of us have experienced driving along and suddenly being jolted into sharp awareness by a sudden stop in traffic ahead of us. We make it to a safe stop and may see that there has been a terrible accident. As we creep around the obstruction we see mangled cars and perhaps a still body being lifted into an ambulance. It registers that lives have been changed in an instant. It gives us pause to reflect on all that we have to be grateful for in our own lives. For a moment we are reminded of how precious life is.

Going through our every day routines we often have a tendency to take the preciousness of life for granted. Not just our own lives, but life in general. We take for granted the oxygen that we breathe, a natural by-product of a balanced environment. Yet our air in general in the world is increasingly more polluted. The Sacramento, California Metropolitan Air Quality Management District states on its website, "...the air districts of El Dorado, Placer, Solano and Yolo counties are part of a designated federal area that doesn't meet the health standard for ozone." Advisories are issued when the Air Quality Index (AQI) for ground-level ozone pollution is forecast to be unhealthy - 150 or over. A recent check showed the index at 100 to 150 in greater Sacramento, and between 151 and 200 in a selected area.

We take for granted the water that we drink and the shelter and safety of our homes. Yet not all people in all parts of the world take these things for granted. As we face the challenges of a burgeoning population, an international financial crisis, a continuing demand for dwindling non-renewable resources, and basic needs being cut while military expenditures increase, there is an ever greater imbalance in the division of material goods and the division of natural resources. Some countries, including the United States, are using far more than a fair share.

To a large degree we have chosen to blind ourselves to the consequences of a taking-for-granted attitude that has exploited non-renewable resources and threatened the health of the planet and the species that inhabit it. The world's resources are declining at an alarming rate. By region, North America consumes 2.7 times the world average, followed by Western Europe, Central and Eastern Europe, the Middle East and Central Asia, Latin America and the Caribbean, Asia and the Pacific, and finally Africa. We cannot afford to take the life of the planet we depend on for granted. We cannot afford to take life for granted. On a personal level and on a collective level, it is a precious gift.

Our ancestors couldn't even imagine the incredible conveniences, abundance and knowledge we have at our fingertips today. By deeply and habitually appreciating the abundance we have and being responsible caretakers of the planet, we create greater satisfaction, balance and peace. As we create a deepening attitude of appreciation and accountability for the resources around us, that influence expands and helps to uplift the world.

If you think you can do a thing or think you can't do a thing, you're right. - Henry Ford

If you want your life to be a magnificent story, then begin by realizing that you are the author and every day you have the opportunity to write a new page. - Mark Houlahan

If I believe I cannot do something, it makes me incapable of doing it. But when I believe I can, then I acquire the ability to do it even if I didn't have it in the beginning. - Mohandas Gandhi

We are what we think - Buddha

No longer do I stay focused on and attract more of what's going wrong, for I've learned to place attention on what's right, what's working, and what's aligned with the All-creating Spirit. - Wayne Dyer

We are shaped by our thoughts; we become what we think. When the mind is pure, joy follows like a shadow that never leaves. - Buddha

A pessimist is one who makes difficulties out of his opportunities, and an optimist is one who makes opportunities of his difficulties. - Harry S. Truman

Human beings can alter their lives by altering their attitudes. - William James

If you realized how powerful your thoughts are you'd never think a negative thought. - Peace Pilgrim

If one advances confidently in the direction of his dreams, and endeavors to live the life which he has imagined, he will meet with a success unexpected in common hours. - Henry David Thoreau

The only limit to our realization of tomorrow will be our doubts of today. - Franklin D. Roosevelt

Treat people as if they were what they ought to be and you help them to become what they are capable of being. - Johann van Goethe

Whatever we expect with confidence becomes our own self-fulfilling prophecy. - Brian Tracy

CHAPTER 3

Expectations Tend to be Realized

It is easy to slip into a habit of negative expectancy without realizing how influential your thoughts are. By focusing on the negative you bring the negative into your present awareness, and the present is the only moment that you actually have to live. When you focus on the positive you stay conscious of the good things that surround you. At any given moment you are choosing to focus your awareness on any number of different aspects of your internal and external experience.

On a simple level, I knew a couple who acquired a new dog, a Scottish Terrier, and named him Rascal. Now ask yourself what image comes to mind when you think or say the name Rascal? Well, the dog obliged and lived up to the expectation in his name. In a fit of frustration over the dog's latest foible, the couple declared that it was time to give the dog a respectful name to live up to. They decided to call him Scotty, imagining a gentlemanly Scotsman. Shortly after being given his new name (with corresponding mental image), the dog's behavior altered into that of a charming companion.

We set up expectancies by the patterns of our thinking or our mental state. If we look at individuals who live in fear of misfortune we see that they are very likely to find it. Job is quoted in the Bible, "That which I feared came upon me." On the other hand, if we look at individuals who seem to be showered with more than their share of good fortune, we discover that such persons have a positive mental expectancy and appreciation of everyday blessings. They are open and receptive to the potential within them and around them. You attract to yourself the things that you focus on.

In times of difficulty or great challenge, the mind that has trained itself in positive directions falls back on that habit. As a dear friend wrote just four weeks after the unexpected and sudden death of her beloved husband, "My great memories over all these years and my gratitude to God for our Countless Blessings is what is getting me through these past weeks." On the other side of the spectrum, a woman in a counseling session had been recounting all the tragedies of her life and relationships. She lamented, "Every morning when I get up I wonder what's going to happen next!" I replied, "Every morning when I get up I marvel at the beauty around me and the potential of this very day. What do you suppose each of us experiences?"

Just as positive thoughts can create positive expectations, negative thoughts can create negative expectations. So who would deliberately create negative expectations? Most of us, actually, and probably more frequently than we realize. Even worry is a kind of negative projection in which we create an awful image of what might or could happen, setting up the possibility for it to happen.

Bruce, for example, had a family history of heart disease. His father and grandfather both died of heart disease before the age of 50. He grew up believing he would himself die young and into adulthood talked about knowing he would die by the age of 50. He ignored all the rules of good health, ignored doctors' advice to lose weight, and had several massive heart attacks by the time he reached 45. He had three things working against him: his hereditary predisposition to heart failure, his belief that he would die early, and his refusal to pay attention to the physical laws of health. We may not be able to quantify the difference it would have made if he had chosen to believe that he could influence his health and increase his longevity by taking advantage of all the advances in health care and preventative lifestyle, but we can predict that he would have added some measure of quality and time.

Bodies have an inherent ability to heal, yet a person's expectations affect that ability. A doctor might set a broken bone, for example, but it is the body itself that knits the broken places back together. It is possible to speed the healing time by adding visualization, if that is within a person's belief system. If, however, a person with a fracture obsesses about a story that was written in the newspaper in which someone's broken bone became infected and festered for years without healing – such obsessed thinking could influence a slowed healing process.

Wayne Dyer describes expectation as a force of attraction. "When I remember to stay in-Spirit, I've realized that when one thing appears to be going wrong, I can see clearly that ten things are going right. For example, if my cell phone isn't working, I can note that my health is fine, my family is safe, the ocean is calm for swimming, by bank account has a surplus, my electricity is fully functional, and on and on it goes. From a perspective of being in-Spirit, I automatically shift my attention away from what's going wrong and attract more of what I'm focused on, whereas at an earlier time in my life, I'd attract more of what was going wrong because that was my point of attraction."

If these ideas seem far-fetched, consider the mind-belief phenomena manifested in the practice of voodoo. In Haiti, where voodoo in some circles is accepted as a cultural belief, I (Cheryl) observed this phenomena first hand when a distressed but otherwise healthy young man came to the clinic where I worked. He was convinced that a voodoo spell had been put on him that would end his life. Over the next days and weeks he began to deteriorate and no amount of reason or treatment convinced him that he could change the outcome. He died with no apparent cause.

Belief and expectation are fascinating reminders of the mind-body connection, as well as the manifestation of events in our lives. When we hold thoughts that diminish us or our potential and focus on them, our own subconscious mind (a reflection of the Universe) believes that is our intention. What we focus on we tend to manifest. If we focus on lack, fear, resentment, or a problem, the Universe reflects back to us in kind. Fill in the blanks in your own life:

I always knew I would ....

I always wanted to .... but ....

Did you do the things you always knew you would? Did you fail to do the things you wanted to but told yourself you couldn't because...? When we recognize how we hold ourselves back we can change the pattern by changing our expectations. When we focus on the greatest possible outcome, we have the capacity to shift into a higher consciousness and potential for positive action and results.

Practices such as hypnotherapy and self-hypnosis allow us to access the subconscious and superconscious, where negative patterns of thinking can be reframed into the creation of positive ones. As the expression goes, change your mind and you change your life. Any practice that connects us to the deeper aspects of mind opens up the potential for growth and healing on every level - physical, mental, emotional and spiritual. Done on a regular basis, such positive changes become automatic and lasting.

Our personal dispositions are as window panes through which we see the world either as rosy or dull. The way we color the glasses we wear is the way the world seems to us. - Fulton J. Sheen

The secret of the man who is universally interesting is that he is universally interested. - William Dean Howells

Man stands in his own shadow and wonders why it is dark. -Ancient Zen saying

Picture yourself as vividly defeated and that alone will make victory impossible. - Harry E. Fosdick

When my mind is all made up to be miserable, I stop to consider; and I am convinced that not the world nor the people in it, but only my mind can make me miserable - or happy. - Fred Van Amburgh

An elephant can be tethered by a thread - if he believes he is captive. If we believe we are chained by habit or anxiety, we are in bondage. - John H. Crowe

A lake that is absolutely calm gives to you a perfect reflection. The moment it becomes disturbed in the least, the reflection is distorted; and if the agitation is increased, the reflection will be completely lost. Your consciousness is the lake. - James B. Schafer

Courage is the price that life exacts for granting peace. The soul that knows it not, knows no release from little things; knows not the livid loneliness of fear, nor mountain heights where bitter joy can hear the sound of wings. - Amelia Earhart

Fear is the main source of superstition, and one of the main sources of cruelty. To conquer fear is the beginning of wisdom. - Bertrand Russell

If the doors of perception were cleansed everything would appear to man as it is, infinite. For man has closed himself up, till he sees all things thru' chinks of his cavern. - William Blake

It's a great thriller or mystery, but on another level it's a film about the fact that, if you only look at a person through one lens, or only believe what you're told, you can often miss the truth that is staring you in the face. - Kevin Spacey

CHAPTER 4

The Lenses We See Through

We begin forming perceptions very early in life that color the way we view ourselves and the world. These lenses, as we can call these early perceptions, influence our reactions and behavior. Whether we are born into a family that is religious or not religious, rich or poor, prejudiced, racially mixed, strict or permissive, the circumstances of our birth and early childhood form much of the basis of our lenses. These lenses often continue to influence us throughout our lives, or until we recognize that we can change a particular lens or perception if it doesn't serve our growing sense of reality.

Let's say that we grow up with a perception of God as a vengeful, punishing male figure who will cut off his love on a whim if we don't please him. This lens may cause some of us to grow up with a fear-based perception of life in which we unconsciously stifle our self-expression and never feel good enough. When anything goes wrong or something bad happens we may think we've done something wrong.

Then we meet someone who perceives God as an unconditionally loving spirit – an impersonal, ever-present force that motivates everything in the universe toward balance and harmony. This person has a compassionate-based perception of life that is motivated by self-expression and exudes confidence. We recognize this as a much more empowering view of the world and, if not too stifled by our fear-based earlier perceptions, begin to feel the stirrings of an inner knowing that resonates toward a more profound perception of ourselves and life. "The mind," said

John Milton, "is its own place and in itself can make a heaven of hell, and a hell of heaven."

An experiment was done many years ago to demonstrate the powerful impact our perceptions have in creating reality. When a group of educationally handicapped children were sent to summer camp, the teachers and counselors at the camp were told that the children were exceptional. Because the teachers believed the children to be exceptional the children responded by opening up to new levels of competence and participation. The results were startling to everyone involved as the children accepted and acted on the perception of themselves as exceptional.

On a more unconscious level, several people looking at the same object will see it differently. A carpenter observing a chair, for example, might see the construction while an artist might see the symmetry and flow. A life counseling seminar leader, Hal Isen, does an interesting exercise with groups to demonstrate how we are influenced by the particular lenses we see through. He has a volunteer come up to the front of the class. A hat with slips of paper is passed around to the other members of the group. Each slip of paper has the name of some occupation on it - psychologist, linguist, nurse, engineer, beautician and so on. Each member is asked to pay attention to a conversation between Hal and the volunteer through the lens of the occupation they have picked out. Afterwards different participants from the audience share what they noticed from their unique perspective. Observing things from a particular perspective is not only interesting, but broadens our understanding of the lenses through which we and others see ourselves and the world.

Our particular lens affects not only the way we experience the world but how the world responds to us. As an example, when a very ordinary man became president of a large bank few people could understand how he came to that position. He had no particular connections or influence, and yet he made the transition from clerk to bank president in a fairly short period of time. Asked by a close friend the secret of his success, he replied that from the moment he began his employment he imagined himself as the president. When he waited on customers and as he went about his daily tasks, he imagined doing his work as though he were already the president. He wasn't aggressive or pushy, he just let the energy of that image of himself as president flow through him. When the president, an elderly man, retired, this ordinary man was elected the new president.

Watching actors in great roles is another way to begin to understand the power of the lenses we see through. Think of Ben Kingsley in the classic movie, Gandhi. As the actor projected himself into the character he seemed to become Gandhi himself, even in physical appearance. Or Meryl Streep, in her powerful performance in Sophie's Choice, as the dysfunctional survivor of the horrors of a concentration camp. Great actors see through the lenses of the characters they portray, temporarily seeming to become them.

Changing the lenses we see through can be powerful, as well as fun to experiment with. Consciously directed visualization can be a powerful form of self-hypnosis, with much greater results than unconscious daydreaming. The next time you have an opportunity to join an unfamiliar group of people, choose ahead of time the image you want to project and really visualize and imagine being that image. Then notice what happens. Do you want to be a leader, full of confidence and ideas? Or do you want to be an interested student or a quiet observer? Get the idea of how you want to present yourself clearly in mind and imagine yourself through this lens. "I think, therefore I am." Then observe the way you are received in the group. Use this technique to challenge any limiting belief that holds you back from doing the things you want to do. By consciously directing the lenses you see yourself through, you can become the person you want to be.

To be blind is bad, but worse it is to have eyes and not to see. - Helen Keller

Life is too brief to waste even one moment in useless or vain expectation. - Dorothy Strange

Change your thoughts and you change your world. - Norman Vincent Peale

Sorrow fully accepted brings its own gifts, for there is alchemy in sorrow. It can be transmuted into wisdom, which, if it does not bring joy, can yet bring happiness. - Pearl S. Buck

Of all the creatures on earth, only human beings can change their patterns. Man alone is the architect of his destiny. Human beings, by changing the inner attitudes of their minds, can change the outer aspects of their lives. - William James

It is when we're given choice that we sit with the gods and design ourselves. - Dorothy Gilman

I read and walked for miles at night along the beach, writing bad blank verse and searching endlessly for someone wonderful who would step out of the darkness and change my life. It never crossed my mind that that person could be me. - Anna Quindlen

It's never too late - in fiction or in life - to revise. - Nancy Thayer

Finish each day and be done with it. You have done what you could; some blunders and absurdities have crept in; forget them as soon as you can. Tomorrow is a new day; you shall begin it serenely and with too high a spirit to be encumbered with your old nonsense - Ralph Waldo Emerson

Forgiveness is an act of the imagination. It dares you to imagine a better future, one that is based on the blessed possibility that your hurt will not be the final word on the matter. It challenges you to give up your destructive thoughts about the situation and to believe in the possibility of a better future. It builds confidence that you can survive the pain and grow from it. - Larry James

If I hold a grudge because I'm angry, I feel strong. But to set that anger aside takes real strength. - Everett L. Worthington, Jr.

CHAPTER 5

Reframing

Reframing is a conscious choice you can make to change your negative or pessimistic attitudes into positive ones. With awareness of your habit patterns you can teach yourself to develop positive perspectives about your past experiences and current circumstances. And you can anticipate the brighter side of things: "Maybe this is the day I'll get that raise!" Rather than the flip side, "I never expect anything, that way I'm not disappointed."

When you feel discomfort, whether it is mental, emotional or physical, it's tempting to give that discomfort more power than all the parts of you that are feeling all right. In fact the purpose of discomfort is usually to get your attention so that you can do whatever is necessary to take care of yourself or address the issue. Then once you've done all you can, you can redirect your focus and action into the task at hand or areas that bring a sense of fulfillment or enjoyment, or just take a moment to appreciate the beauty of the sky as the sun sets, or the radiant glow of flowers at dusk, or the love of family, friends and home.

Most of us have gotten stuck in patterns of negativity at some time. Various ways of being or habits have even been passed down from earlier generations that have held onto hardships or pessimistic views: "I had to walk five miles to school in the snow and rain," as the old stories went. It wasn't that long ago that life was very limited compared to the present. Several generations ago, some individuals might be born, live and die, all within the small radius of a few miles around a family's home or town. People were dependent upon walking wherever they wanted to go or they might have a horse and buggy to get the five miles into town. Nowadays, if you have to take a bus or train because you can't afford a car, you're living in the comfort of great advances.

Why do we get stuck in patterns of negativity? Habit, mostly, and perhaps lacking the recognition that we are not a product of our feelings, but rather we choose them. You may resist the idea that you are responsible for your feelings but it is true nonetheless. No one outside of you can make you feel bad about yourself unless you let them. If you're feeling down or depressed and someone makes a careless or cutting remark, if you're like most of us, you'll probably feel hurt or mad about it. But if you're feeling confident and on top of the world, the same remark is more likely to bounce right off. In either case, the choice to feel bad or not is your own.

There are any number of underlying causes for patterns of negativity, such as feelings of unworthiness, low self-esteem and insecurity. Deep-seated feelings of not being good enough can undermine many positive thoughts and validate negative ones. As in the example above, if you're not feeling good about yourself and someone pays you a complement you might regard it as flattery rather than truth. "They're just being nice." Or if there is something that you've really been wanting you might think, "I know I don't really deserve it." When you catch yourself falling into attitudes of low self-esteem or negative reactions, you can practice making reframing a habit. If you don't reframe, negativity becomes a more entrenched habit.

The first step in reframing is awareness. You can start paying attention to your thoughts and the words you use when you speak. You can't change something if you aren't aware of it. Listen to the attitude of your thoughts and words. Do you put yourself down? Do you put others down? Experiment with replacing negative thoughts with a positive reframing. The next time you start to think something negative about yourself or someone else, think about something positive and true instead. Notice the difference in your feelings.

A great story that illustrates the power of reframing comes from a woman named Alice, who worked as a teacher's aid in an elementary school. During summer vacation she had been inspired by a woman (the subject of a later chapter) who called herself Peace Pilgrim. Peace talked about the power of thought and seeing ourselves and others from a perspective of compassion. Alice thought about that a lot, especially in regard to a co-worker, who she regarded as very annoying. It wasn't just Alice, most of the other teachers and aids felt the same way. Alice wanted to change the negative thoughts she was having about this woman, and she wanted to change her automatic negative response whenever she came into contact with her. She decided that when the school year started she would reframe her thoughts. Whenever she saw the woman or thought of her, she determined to consciously choose a thought that was positive. And it had to be true or it wouldn't be valid. Even if all she could think was, "Her hair looks nice today," that would suffice. These weren't things she would say out loud, they were just choices she was making in her thoughts.

By the end of the first semester something extraordinary was happening. The annoying woman was relating much better to her environment and her peers. Not just Alice, but other members of the staff were feeling more open and accepting of her. By the end of the year she didn't even stand out. You may think that your thoughts are silent and therefore don't effect those around you. In reality, everything is energy. Thought is subtle energy that gets picked up on some level. You may not consciously be aware of what others are thinking but you do respond, however unconsciously, to the energy or thought patterns around you.

It can be very interesting to pay closer attention to the words you use and the ideas you have about them. You might think that a particular word is positive and yet when you take a closer look you can see that it hooks you into something negative, as in the following examples:

Try: A Gestalt expression is, trying is lying. It implies a kind of built-in acceptance of failure. "Do your best and you'll do fine on the test," says the professor. "I'll try," says the pupil, the response itself suggesting a lack of confidence in a positive outcome.

To reframe: "This has been a challenging subject for me but I've been working really hard and making progress," affirms a positive intention to do well.

Should: The word should comes laden with guilt and judgment. If you don't do the thing you should you're somehow bad or weak. It lays a guilt a trip on the person it's being used toward, whether yourself or someone else. "It's such a beautiful day. I'd love to get outside but I really should clean the house." Think of this expression: Be careful or you'll should all over yourself!

To reframe: "It's a beautiful day. I'd love to get out but I'll enjoy it more if I clean the house first," or "I don't want to miss this beautiful day and I can always clean house tomorrow." A conscious choice without guilt is empowering.

Can't: "I can't do that." If someone is referring to picking up 2000 pounds or speaking a foreign language fluently at first exposure, that would be a valid statement. But "can't" is often used as an excuse not to do something that needs to be done - like break a bad habit or incorporate a good one into your life. To say, "I can't do it," is not taking responsibility. In essence, you're saying that you'll never make an effort. "I can't talk to my father" or "I can't quit smoking."

To reframe: Start by taking responsibility. "I'm not ready to talk to my father" or "I'm not ready to quit smoking." Just taking responsibility for the choice is empowering and will give you more confidence as you get ready to move to the next step: "I'm ready to take this on."

Reframing is a way of consciously choosing to have a meaningful, positive attitude toward life – one of the requisites for healthy and happy living. Even when challenges come, you can choose to put them into a positive perspective: you don't set out to create problems but when they come they contribute to your inner growth. Without them you would simply drift through life. It is through solving problems according to the best you know that you have the opportunity to learn from your mistakes, grow in confidence, and find your strength.

At the center of your being you have unimagined resources. - Lao-Tzu

Within you lies the sea of infinite knowledge and inspiration. - Yogananda

The possibilities of creative effort connected with the subconscious mind are stupendous and imponderable. They inspire one with awe. - Napoleon Hill

The person with a fixed goal, a clear picture of his desire, or an ideal always before him, causes it, through repetition, to be buried deeply in his subconscious mind and is thus enabled, thanks to its generative and sustaining power, to realize his goal in a minimum of time and with a minimum of physical effort. - Claude M. Bristol

It is psychological law that whatever we desire to accomplish we must impress upon the subjective or subconscious mind. - Orison Swett Marden

We must realize that the subconscious mind is the law of action and always expresses what the conscious mind has impressed on it. What we regularly entertain in our mind creates a conception of self. What we conceive ourselves to be, we become. - Grace Speare

Our subconscious minds have no sense of humor, play no jokes and cannot tell the difference between reality and an imagined thought or image. What we continually think about eventually will manifest in our lives. - Robert Collier

The conscious mind may be compared to a fountain playing in the sun and falling back into the great subterranean pool of subconscious from which it rises. - Sigmund Freud

In the creative state a man is taken out of himself. He lets down as it were a bucket into his subconscious, and draws up something which is normally beyond his reach. He mixes this thing with his normal experiences and out of the mixture he makes a work of art. - E. M. Forster

CHAPTER 6

A Positive Understanding of the Subconscious

The rational, intellectual part of the mind is amazing - constantly juggling external information and situations, sorting through facts, making choices and often on fast forward as we muscle our way through the day. It can be rich, stimulating and exhausting all at once. Then we might throw ourselves into some mind-numbing activity like television, social media or internet surfing as a way to relax and put on the breaks. What we may be short-circuiting is our connection to a deeper, inner awareness that links us to our greatest potential.

The subconscious mind, just below the surface, is a rich reservoir of everything that is stored away from our conscious awareness in order to keep us from existing in a confusing chaos of information and complexity that can better be dealt with in small bites. It is the non-reasoning part of the mind that is a storehouse of our previous programming, memories and experiences. It is also the part of the mind that dreams, regulates autonomic body functions, is the pathway to creativity, imagination and intuition, and gateway to the superconscious. Henry David Thoreau tells us, "Direct your eye inward, and you'll find a thousand regions in your mind yet undiscovered."

One of those hidden regions contains a current of creativity. When you connect with the subconscious you access that constantly flowing stream. Fritz Perls said that the average person "lives only five percent to 15 percent of his potential at the highest. A person who has even 25 percent of his potential available is already considered to be a genius." The rest of that 75 to 95 percent is unused potential, accessible when you develop an ongoing connection with the subconscious mind. A look at practices like meditation and self-hypnosis can give a perspective of what can be achieved through a greater understanding of the subconscious.

Meditation, in part, is the practice of silencing the "inner chatter." This mental focusing has a door opening effect that has been described as a clearing of the mind and sharpening of the mental processes. By way of the subconscious mind, the superconscious mind is accessed. A neurologist, Richard Cytowic, tried a form of meditation or quieting of the mind called Zazen. Although he was skeptical, he sat in front of a blank wall until he reached what is called "the still point." He wrote of the experience, "My cognitive mind was astonished that the internal dialogue really could be stopped, while the rest of me relished the sense of tranquility that accompanied this feat. It is a feeling (that) must be experienced to be understood, because it cannot be explained." A poll published in Newsweek stated that 45 percent of meditators polled had "sensed the sacred" while meditating.

What does all of this mean in terms of the affect of meditation on daily life? It can lower blood pressure and stress levels, lead to clearer thinking, more energy, and a sense of connection with something spiritual or bigger than ourselves. The affects differ between individuals and range from calming to mountain-top or peak experiences. One woman who was taught meditation and relaxation techniques while in the hospital felt so peaceful and loving that she wanted to share it with others. She walked down the hall and found a woman sitting by herself in a room. As they talked she observed the other woman's spirits lift. It happened with the woman's roommate as well. She called it the rippling effect, a feeling of being saturated in love.

The state of relaxation can be expanded with hypnosis and hypnotic processes. Relaxation and deepening allow our awareness to pass through that door to the subconscious where positive suggestions and visualization can become very powerful and healing. Old negative habit patterns can be uprooted and replaced with positive new ones. On an even deeper and therapeutic level, misconceptions or negative beliefs held by the subconscious may be brought to the surface where they can be processed, education can be given, and the subconscious programmed with new information and empowered beliefs.

In the late 19th century the term "unconscious" was used to refer to the part of the mind that is out of sight of rational awareness. One school of thought brought to the forefront by Sigmund Freud was that the unconscious was comprised of negative forces that attempt to break through into consciousness and have to be controlled. However, as the field of hypnotherapy developed, gradually more practitioners began to use the term subconscious and emphasize it as a positive force that could be directed and trained.

Hypnosis is an altered and natural state beyond ordinary consciousness that can occur spontaneously. In addition, there are many ways that hypnosis can be induced and deepened. A spontaneous form of hypnosis is entered when we get absorbed in some activity or thought process to such a degree that we momentarily lose awareness of our environment. It might happen while reading a book or watching television or even "highway hypnosis" while driving a car. We simply narrow our focus to an activity or thought that is all-engrossing.

An eclectically trained hypnotherapist can use a variety of methods to bring a person into a state of hypnosis, deepen and lighten the state, guide various processes and return the subject back to normal awareness. Generally, the most well known characteristic of hypnosis is increased suggestibility. Though there are varying degrees of this heightened responsiveness to suggestion, it is only one of many kinds of value that can result from access to the subconscious. It is used in areas such as chronic and acute pain control, to change the pain threshold or to affect the psychological associations of pain. It can be used effectively to improve confidence, concentration, recall, motivation, achievement, focus, health and stress management. Hypnosis can help overcome addictions, habits, eating disorders, insomnia, fears, phobias, negative thought, emotional and behavior patterns. It can also tap people into the utilization of their full potential in endeavors like work, sports, art or creative expression.

By definition, any method that gives you direct access to your subconscious or inner mind while awake is hypnotic. Whenever profound therapy takes place, it is the result of entering an altered state that accesses and affects the subconscious mind, whether induction is formal or spontaneous. Understanding the subconscious mind as a positive force that can be directed and trained allows you the greatest use of this inherent creative potential, providing access to an empowered life of meaning and fulfillment.

We say, "it's only imagination," yet through the practice of imagination, we can help to heal our bodies and move towards the manifestation of our heart's desires. As Tagore said, with a poet's insight, "the stronger the imagination, the less imaginary the results." – Author Unknown

Every moment of your life you are creating through thought. You create your own inner conditions and you're helping to create the conditions around you. -Peace Pilgrim

Any activity becomes creative when the doer cares about doing it right, or better. – John Updike

Thoughts of strength both build strength from within and attract it from without. Thoughts of weakness actualize weakness from within and attract it from without. - Ralph W. Trine

Great men are they who see that spiritual is stronger than any material force, that thoughts rule the world. - Emerson

What we sow or plant in the soil will come back to us in exact kind. It is impossible to sow corn and get a crop of wheat, but we entirely disregard this law when it comes to mental sowing. - Orison Swett Marden

The greatest achievement was at first and for a time a dream. The oak sleeps in the acorn; the bird waits in the egg; and in the highest vision of the soul, a waking angel stirs. - James Allen

A mind that is stretched to a new idea never returns to its original dimensions. – Albert Einstein

Whatever you believe you can do, or dream you can, begin it. Boldness has genius, power and magic to it. – Goethe

The future belongs to those who believe in the beauty of their dreams. - Eleanor Roosevelt

To accomplish great things, we must not only act but also dream, not only plan but also believe. – Anatole France

By believing passionately in that that doesn't exist, we create it. - Wayne Dyer

CHAPTER 7

The Creative Power of Thought

Thought is a function of mind and to fully utilize this most precious of gifts, it serves us well to understand the complexity of our cognitive potential. The conscious mind is the reasoning mind. It contains the seat of our will power, discipline, discernment, discrimination and concentration. The conscious mind can be likened to a computer programmer, the part that directs and makes decisions.

Like a computer, the subconscious mind is the storehouse of our prior programming. As mentioned in the previous chapter, it is a memory bank of our thoughts, feelings, emotions, memories, imagination, creativity, habit patterns, impulses, desires and instincts. It includes that automatic part of our mind that operates the physical body without any conscious direction. The subconscious mind can also be called a gateway to the superconscious.

The superconscious mind is our source of greater awareness. It connects us to that place of intuition and inner guidance as well as to the collective unconscious, a vast reservoir of information that can be accessed through this channel.

When you begin to understand more fully the almost limitless boundaries of your mind, you can use your tremendous creative potential to create a more rich and empowered life, filled with purpose and meaning. In order to successfully make positive changes you need to use more than the conscious mind or seat of will power, which may be in conflict with deeply held patterns or beliefs in the subconscious mind. When you make a connection with the underlying aspects of mind, you are able to reach and affect deeply held patterns and beliefs for the purpose of reeducation and facilitating permanent change.

A decision utilizing the conscious mind alone is an act of will and though it may work in the short term, it usually doesn't affect the level at which habits reside. Therefore an individual may intellectually decide to quit smoking, but unless he or she reaches down into the subconscious mind and makes a shift at the source, the force of the habit is more likely to resurface. By utilizing tools which access our subconscious minds, such as imagination and emotion, we can get to the source and change a habit pattern or unconscious belief, which is the basis of hypnotherapy and self-hypnosis.

In order to use the full potential of your thoughts you need to get past any limiting beliefs that have held you back or blocked your ability to create the rich and empowered life of your choosing. Your core beliefs are predominantly the product of ideas taken in from the influences around you when you were young, before you had developed a reasoning mind of your own, and those you continued to take on as a result of your experiences as you grew. You may even hold conflicting beliefs which cause you to wonder why you seem to sabotage yourself or have difficulty following through with an intention.

Let's say your intention is to be successful in business but you keep holding back instead of trying to get that promotion. In may be that a conflicting belief is being held in the subconscious mind, perhaps that you are incapable or don't deserve what you desire. Where do such disempowering perceptions or misconceptions come from and how do you get rid of them? Processes like hypnosis and meditation allow you to tap into a greater pool of your mind potential, enabling you to uncover and uproot disempowering beliefs. Then you can get the power of your creative mind behind you to create empowering beliefs that enable you to move forward.

Once you have created an empowered belief system, the first step of any desired change is to define your intention. What is it that you wish to change? When you make the changes you desire, what do the changes look like? Visualization or imagination is a powerful step in the process of creating positive change and direction. It can be especially powerful in helping to break down habits that have held you back in some way. Let's say you're a procrastinator. There are many things that you want to do, that you plan to do, but you rarely get to them. And you don't understand why, so you berate yourself, feel guilty, and stay immobilized.

How can you use the creative power of your thoughts to break this pattern? A first step would be to define your intention. What are the things that you want to accomplish but have not acted on? It's important to state your intention clearly. It may be that you're unhappy in your present position at work. You want to stay with the company that you've invested your time and energy in, but you want to move up into a better position. And you want to make more money so that you can move into a home that meets your family's growing needs.

This is as far as you may normally get in your thinking before becoming overwhelmed and immobilized. This is not the place to stop, but the place to begin creative thinking. You need to determine if these are realistic goals. If they are not, they need to be modified. It's important to get fully behind your belief in the possibilities. Then you can look at what steps are needed to move in that direction. Perhaps it will be necessary to take several courses in order to qualify for that promotion or there may be special training to look into. Or it may mean finding the courage to speak up, confidently, to your boss.

Next, it's time to visualize what the outcome of that intention looks like. In your mind you can imagine signing up for that class or training. You can see yourself successfully completing the program. You can imagine yourself speaking confidently to your boss and being congratulated on actually getting the desired position. In your mind's eye you can go through a day performing your new duties. The more you engage your emotions, practice feeling confident and excited and being good at this work, the more empowering the visualization will be in manifesting the desired outcome. You can imagine your new paycheck and feel the satisfaction. You can look around in your imagination and find an ideal house that would best suit the family's needs, and take time to enjoy being there. Still in your state of creative thinking, you can look back at all the steps it took to get to this place.

These steps can be applied to any desired skill or goal: public speaking, confidence, concentration, athletic or scholastic achievement, enhanced relationships. The following is a general outline of steps that can be contracted or expanded or changed in any way that fits a personal goal:

Create an empowered belief system. If a belief is holding you back in any way, it is disempowering. Change the belief by substituting an empowered one. Example: Change from, "I've never been comfortable in new situations," to "I'm ready and excited to embrace new situations and the rewarding experiences and adventures to come."

State an intention: What is it that you want to accomplish or change? Be as specific as possible. "I want to lose weight" is general. "I want to weigh 135 pounds and be radiantly healthy" is more specific.

Check the goals. Are they realistic? (Not, "Am I confident enough?" But, "If I want to become a teacher am I willing to put in the time and effort to get through school, etc.")

If necessary, modify goals to be realistic. Get beliefs fully behind the intention that is set.

List all of the steps it will take to get to the realization of the goal.

Visualize. Engage your emotions. See yourself successfully accomplishing each step you have listed and notice how good the accomplishment feels at every step along the way. You may discover more steps to add to your list.

Let your imagination play with the fantasy of your goal already being accomplished. Begin acting as if you are already there.

Step by step, move your visualizations into action. Modify when necessary.

Research and science show the validity of the mind-body connection. The reality is that we are not hardwired to be a certain way for the duration of our lives and our genes do not pre-determine a certain path or outcome. We are constantly adapting and changing. The creative power of our thinking gives us tremendous ability to shift from powerless to powerful by changing the way we think.

Intention, the first step in goal setting, is general. It enables us to connect to universal energy, which is amazingly powerful. Wayne Dyer calls intention the spiritual aspect of goal setting. There are seven words he used to represent this connection to that higher directing force: creativity, kindness, love, beauty, expansion, abundance and receptivity. If we feel or behave inconsistently with these seven facets of intention, he says, we've disconnected from the power of intention. That means we're on our own - without those powerful universal forces.

When we enter this elevated place of working with intention we have an opportunity to examine any and all self-imposed obstacles. These are the limiting beliefs or misconceptions we have that can hold us back from setting our intentions and achieving our goals.

Once we see a negative thought pattern or belief we can recognize it as a disempowering thought and replace it with an empowering one. What we focus on, we tend to manifest. As you become aware of your inner dialogue you can ask yourself these questions: are these thoughts empowering or disempowering? Am I in charge or a victim? Am I coming from fear or compassion? By becoming aware we are able to reframe our thinking to a positive perspective. As inspirations come from this elevated state they can then be put into action. Without action they become unrealized potential. As we act on our inspirations doors we may not have even anticipated can begin to open. Positive inner dialogue becomes the link connecting us to intention, and intention leads to inspiration and action.

Research shows that with the conscious direction of thought things beyond the ordinary are created, beyond even what was thought possible - within the boundaries of reality. We live in a vast field of potential. We can use our minds with deliberate intention, as a powerful creative tool. We can lift our awareness from the restrictions of our ordinary reality into that universal force, surpassing the confines of formerly limited perceptions.

Start with your creative imagination, and imagine looking through a special window that allows you to see right to the source of all creation. You yourself are connected to this source, this limitless energy. Your intention is to stay connected, to live your life on purpose, open to the inspiration of your own higher nature. Feel the dormant forces come alive. As you begin putting your focus on the positive things that you'd really like to see happen in your life, you may be surprised at what you can actually do.

As a single footstep will not make a path on earth, so a single thought will not make a pathway in the mind. To make a deep physical path, we walk again and again. To make a deep mental path, we must think over and over the kind of thoughts we wish to dominate our lives. - Henry David Thoreau

Negative thinking must be treated like any addiction, with commitment to life, patience, discipline, a will to get better, forgiveness, and the knowledge that recovery is not just possible but, following certain guidelines, inevitable. - Peter McWilliams and John-Roger

People are always blaming circumstances for what they are. I don't believe in circumstances. The people who get on in this world are the people who get up and look for the circumstances they want, and if they can't find them, make them. – George Bernard Shaw

If you realized how powerful your thoughts are, you would never think a negative thought. They can have powerful influence for good when they're on the positive side, and they can and do make you physically ill when they're on the negative side. – Peace Pilgrim

It is not the place, nor the condition, but the mind alone that can make anyone happy or miserable. - Roger L'Estrange

Whatever we accomplish in this world we accomplish through the power of concentration, which is nothing but meditation. Above all, meditation stills the wandering mind and establishes us forever in a state of peace. - Swami Muktananda

Every good thought you think is contributing its share to the ultimate result of your life. - Grenville Kleiser

If we only knew how deeply, absolutely, that our smallest act, our smallest thought, has such far-reaching effects; setting forces in motion; reaching out to the galaxy; how carefully we would act and speak and think. How precious life would become in its integral wholeness. – Irina Tweedie

One's own thought is one's world. What a person thinks is what he becomes – that is the eternal mystery. – The Upanishads

My life has been filled with terrible misfortune, most of which never happened. – Mark Twain

CHAPTER 8

Overcoming Negative Thinking

In any given moment you have free will as to what you choose to focus on, and in any given moment you can choose to focus on something positive. In this fast and furious, sometimes chaotic world, however, it is not uncommon to find ourselves drawn into the black hole of negative thoughts and feelings. It isn't surprising that the term road rage has become a common expression. You may be on your way to work or to an engagement or appointment and you find yourself bumper to bumper in stop and go traffic. You can succumb to a reaction of stress - a few choice words under your breath, a quickening of heart rate and pulse, "black cloud thoughts" and so on. But this reaction is by no means necessary or pre-ordained. It is a choice, or perhaps in part the result of a negative habit. If you want to reduce your stress level at any given moment, you can change the thoughts you are thinking. Not so simple? Actually, it can be.

The next time you get caught in a traffic jam and notice those negative thoughts and that elevated blood pressure, change the stream of your thoughts. If you think it can't be done, do it anyway. Ask yourself this question: Is there anything I can do at this minute to change the situation? Maybe you can turn at the next light or turnoff and take another route. If it's out of your hands take some slow, deep breaths, which automatically begins to slow down your autonomic body functions – including heart rate and pulse. Choose something pleasant to think about. Or something funny. It's healthy. You might listen to some music or make eye contact with the person in the car next to you and smile. Challenge yourself to change your focus to something positive and feel the high that comes from taking charge and turning a stressful situation into one in which you feel empowered.

Rita, a student in a hypnotherapy class, was dealing with an extreme issue of road rage. Her negative attitude and actions were escalating and her husband was concerned that her reactions would put her in danger. In hypnosis she revealed that rage was a response she had cultivated while growing up, in situations in which she felt powerless. It was also modeled by her father. After a comprehensive session of regression hypnotherapy she made some big changes. (The session in its entirety can be read in Catharsis in Regression Hypnotherapy: Transcripts of Transformation by Randal Churchill.)

A few weeks after her session, Rita told the class that she was feeling more flexible. "It's an overall feeling of spaciousness and less need to control. I feel less that I have to control other people when I'm driving." She admitted to still reacting with irritation to other drivers and still making knee-jerk comments like, "Nice going!" but without the intensity of feeling she had before. Then she tried an experiment to change her experience even more. She decided to be "really generous" to other drivers, just to see what it was like. So she would motion people to go ahead of her, even if she felt she was being cut off and say, "Go ahead." And people responded with smiles and waves. She realized how much better that felt. It was so much more empowering than her previous anger.

Another common habit of negative thinking has to do with worry or anxiety. Worry or anxiety is usually over something in the past that can't be changed or a projection into the future that hasn't even happened. Either way we are losing energy in the present and creating unhappiness for ourselves. The Gestalt definition of anxiety is the gap between the now and the projected future that doesn't exist.

Worry and anxiety are habits that result in a negative mulling over of events or circumstances in a way that goes nowhere and drains energy. Concern, on the other hand, is a positive energy which motivates us to take some action. We can either take action to amend some consequence from the past or forgive a transgression made against us or by us, and move on. If the concern is for something that hasn't happened yet, we can take steps in the present that will have a positive influence on the future.

In striving to overcome negative thinking patterns you can accept that you don't deliberately create or seek out difficult experiences, but when they come you can turn them into empowering learning experiences. Another perspective to consider is that everything that comes to you in life comes for a reason. If you choose to see things that way you empower yourself to find a positive angle in any situation, no matter how challenging.

Depression is another example. In the book *Emotionally Free*, psychiatrist David Viscott points out that depression can be a sign that you can't afford to ignore the longing of your heart any longer. This perspective reframes the pain of depression into an opportunity to pay attention to what's going on in your life, and make some changes. Depression may be a sign that something is going on, such as a loss of some kind. A depressed person might ask, "What did I lose?" "On a scale of one to ten, how important was it?" The next question might be something like, "What might I have done differently?" Not in order to be judgmental or blaming toward yourself, but to notice whether or not there was something you could have done in a different way.

A lost relationship, for example, could lead to depression. That would answer the first question, "What was lost?" If the loss has led to chronic depression, then on a scale of one to ten, the importance of that loss has to be up near the top. Now the important soul-searching question. What might I have done differently? Put away the disempowering (victim) perspective and look at your own actions or reactions – or lack of action when action was needed. Soul-searching requires the willingness to be absolutely honest with yourself.

Very often, if you've seen yourself as the victim in a situation, you can take your power back by assigning appropriate responsibility to your part: If the partner I expected to spend my life with abandoned/cheated on/humiliated me and chose to leave or break up the relationship, what was my role?

Were there ways that I might have acted differently in the relationship? Were there times that I might have taken my partner for granted or been unsupportive? Or were there times when my partner took me for granted or was unsupportive and I didn't take responsibility for speaking up in an appropriate way or asking for what I needed? Were there times when I could have acted and I did nothing? At that first sign of (physical/emotional) abuse I could have gotten help or left. When I sat home wondering where my partner was I might have spoken up and gotten clear or gotten counseling.

In a different situation of loss, say the death of a spouse or loved on, you can still look at your actions, your reactions, and the times when you might have acted and didn't. In that inner quiet place or self-hypnosis you can look at whether you feel you took responsibility for your actions and feelings in the relationship with your loved one. Is there anything that you left unsaid or undone? You can use self or hetero hypnosis or a journal to "talk out" whatever comes up. It might simply be that you've lost that feeling of connection, which you can still find if you get quiet and go inside. With openness and receptivity we can emotionally connect with our loved ones who have gone on and sense that our unhappiness or depression in some way affects them, too. In this case, depression can be used as a reminder to consciously re-focus on positive memories, good times shared, and a renewed sense of connection.

If you can use your negative thoughts, whatever form they take, as a time of mental housecleaning and remind yourself of the strengths that have pulled you through tough times in the past, you have the potential to transform and express your thoughts in a positive direction that your life will follow.

The Star Guy: A Lesson in Positive Thinking

I (Cheryl) first saw the "Star Show" at a Home and Garden Fair in a local city. Small groups of people were ushered into a trailer set up with bench seats all around the interior. Once seated the lights were turned off and stars lit up the ceiling. It was beautiful. For a reasonable price the artist would come to your home and paint a constellation of stars that represented any date of your choosing on the ceiling of a room. What a great concept, I thought.

Two years later I purchased a two-story geodesic dome with a cupola on the third floor – a small, five-sided room with windows facing out in every direction. Looking up at the slightly rounded ceiling I knew it was the perfect room for those stars. I searched the internet, looking for any company in the area that painted stars. I couldn't remember the name of the artist from the home show or his company, and I didn't find anything. It stayed in the back of my mind, just out of sight. Then one drizzly Sunday morning I saw an ad online for a Home and Garden Show in that same city. It was taking place on that very day. On impulse, I decided to go.

When I arrived at the event, booths were spread out in every direction. I picked up a flyer on the table that listed all of the booths. I looked through it for any name with "stars" in it. Almost to the end, and nothing. Then there it was – Star Gazer! I was so excited to find it.

The trailer was set up in the same way it had been. A group of people were ushered in and sat down. The lights turned off and the stars came out. When the lights came on again everyone was beaming. I signed up to have the stars painted at my home and put down my deposit. The young woman taking applications said the artist was booked for almost three months, but then he would call to make an appointment.

I called the star guy just before three months was up and got his answering machine. I left a message. He called back. I liked his voice. He said he would call again in a couple of days and set a date. I told him about a special celebration I was having at the dome in a couple of weeks and hoped he could come out before that. He said he could. It was spring and beautiful this time of year – the hills were green and the lake behind the house was full.

When I didn't hear from the star guy I left another message. When he got back to me he told me that his van had been broken into and all of his equipment was stolen. It was going to take time to replace everything and he had some things on order. He would be in touch. His equipment didn't arrive in time for the celebration, but I hoped it would come before the holidays. It didn't.

Finally – the star guy called. A date was set. I was thrilled. I cautioned him that the stairway leading to the cupola was narrow and that the opening on the top was more like entering a cave. He would have to bend down to get through, then once inside the ceiling was eight feet high. He said that would be fine. When he arrived he extended his hand. "I'm Greg," he said. He was a big guy. Six feet easily, and stocky. And wearing a knee brace. I wondered how he would ever get himself and his equipment up the stairs and through the low entrance to the cupola!

He entered the dome and looked around with wide eyes. "Wow! This place is so cool!" It was pretty unique and I was glad he was enjoying it. Then he spotted Socrates and headed right over to pet him. "What a great cat," he said, with obvious sincerity.

Then he saw Missy, and headed over to pet her. (I was already impressed. My formerly feral cats didn't usually allow strangers to pet them.)

"I've got six of them at home," he told me and launched into his first story. He had one cat, and then an abandoned cat showed up. He felt sorry for her and took her in. He hadn't realized she was pregnant but then she had four kittens. Hence he now had six. He didn't mention why he had kept them all but he went on, telling about the raccoon couple who came into his yard and had babies the same time the kittens were born. The kittens and baby raccoons grew up together and got along. They even ate together. When one of the raccoons got hit by a car in the street he went out to pick it up. It had hurt its shoulder but it was alive. He carried it in his arms to his back yard and called the animal shelter to pick it up. They were going to relocate it after it healed. They came with a stick with a loop at the end that was supposed to drop around its neck. "Hey!" he said. "If you had kids would you use that on them?" And he went over and picked the raccoon up in his arms. "Be careful," he was warned. "That's a wild animal. It could have rabies." He placed it gently in the cage. It was later tested for rabies, but the test was negative.

I took Greg up into the cupola, relieved when he pushed his equipment through the opening and easily fit through himself. "Did you injure your knee," I asked? "I noticed your brace." "Yeah, I injured it while training on my night job," he said. "I catch bad guys at night. I just went through the police academy." Then looking around, "Wow! What a cool room!" I showed him the black corkboard trimmed in felt that I had cut out to fit the windows to block daylight. I wanted to be able to show the stars during the day as well as at night. He was surprised and said no one had done that before. I left him to do his star thing while I worked in my office on the floor below. He worked for quite some time and then came down the stairs to get something. I don't remember how the stories started, or even what order he told them in, but he held me spellbound.

"I was a football player in high school," he began, which considering his size and bulk made sense. "I used to go to the field a couple of hours before a game and lay on my back on the grass. I would feel the grass, smell the grass. Then I would picture the game in my mind. I didn't see faces, but I would see the plays as they happened. Then when it came time to play my teammates would be focused and tense. I was pretty relaxed. I played hard and enjoyed the game.

"Then I injured my neck and I started to get migraine headaches. They were really bad and it went on for more than a year. I went to a doctor and he did an MRI to see what was going on. When I went in for the results he said, 'Come in and close the door.' Uh, oh, I thought. What's going on. He turned out the lights and showed me the x-rays. 'See all this damage here? You're not going to ever play football again.' I opened the door. See you later, Doc. I've got three games left to play. Then I'll come back to see you.

"So I played the next two games. Then I went to the field, like always, before the third game and laid on my back on the grass. I smelled the grass and felt it in my fingers and started to picture the game in my mind. Then I saw myself on my back looking up. Lots of people were looking down at me saying, 'Are you all right, Greg?' That picture wouldn't get out of my head so before the game I went to the coach and asked him to send a player out in my place for the first part of the game. Someone who would like the opportunity to play. 'Are you kidding?' he said. I said no, send someone out in my place. So he did. Then I went in for the second half and I played cautiously – which I didn't usually do. I got through the game all right and after that I went to the doctor. He did surgery on my neck but I still got migraines and was stiff. He told me I'd never do certain things again.

"I went to another doctor. He said, 'Greg, you can do anything you want to do. We just need to fix this problem.' I said, you're talking my language. He did a second surgery on my neck and from the time I woke up from the anesthesia I never had a migraine again.

"I learned a lot in life from playing football. It wasn't the game itself, it was what my coaches taught me. I was given so much and I want to give back. I really want to help people. Do you know the four P's?" he asked me. I admitted I did not. "I used to teach it to the kids, teaching them how to get what they really want in life. Let's see if I can remember: Picture, plan, practice, and persist.

"What do you really like to do, I would ask. For me, I like to shop. And I really like to buy good suits. So when I go through a mall and I see a great suit I stop and picture myself in it. I close my eyes and I can feel the texture in my imagination. I can tell if it's wool or a cotton blend. I can feel the cut of the suit on my body. I like an athletic cut. I see myself wearing the suit. Then I ask myself, is it practical? Something I'm really going to wear? I think of an event I will wear it to. If it is practical, then I make a plan. How much is the suit, what do I need to do to get it. Then I persist until the goal is reached. If I want to do it, I can do it.

"I've had various jobs in my life and I always go in knowing that I can reach the top. I got this one job where I started as a supervisor. Right away I told the guys working for me that I wanted to train a couple of them to take my place because I planned on moving up. No one was up for it. They didn't want to work more hours even though the pay would be much better. They were content to stay where they were, not putting in too much effort and not moving ahead. I told a friend of mine, 'I bet I could take someone right off the street, someone motivated, and train them to be a better supervisor than any of these guys.' He laughed.

"Then I was getting gas across the street and this young man came up and asked if he could wash my windows for 50 cents. I got to talking with him and asked if washing windows was solely what he did or if he did anything else. He said he unloaded trucks when the truckers came in. He lived on the street, sleeping under bridges and in a shelter sometimes. When he finished the windows I saw that he had done a really good job. I gave him a dollar and said, I see that you really did your best on these windows. Then I pointed to the building across the street and said, that's where I work. If you're interested and you really want to change your life, come over tomorrow at three o'clock and talk to me about a job. He came by the next day and he really wanted to work. I showed him around and told him what the other guys didn't want to do. He was willing to do the work and he did his best. I talked to him about getting a bicycle to get to work on and helped him pick one out. He showed up regularly and worked hard. Later I talked to him about buying a car and then helped him to get an apartment. When I was ready to move up he was ready to be supervisor. In time I left but he's still there and doing very well."

"How did you get into the star business?" I asked him. "Well, I was a customer. I saw this demonstration and I wanted to have the stars in my room. The owner sent over this woman who worked for him and she asked me to pick a date for the night sky I would like to have on my ceiling. I gave her a favorite date in August. She painted the stars and she didn't do a great job but it was okay. It was just a job to her.

"My friend came over and thought it was cool. He had studied astronomy and I told him that it was an August night sky. He laughed. He pointed out that it was not. The North star wasn't in the north and it wasn't an August night sky. I was mad and called the owner. He said, 'What do you want me to do? Do you want your money back or what?' I said, when you get ready to sell your business I want to buy it. I could do a much better job. Two years later he called me. He said, 'I remembered what you said and I'm ready to sell my business.' I had worked my way up in the job I was at and was doing quite well but I was ready to move on. I told my boss I was leaving and starting my own business. He was surprised and said, 'What are you going to do?' I told him I was going to paint stars and he laughed and said, 'I thought you were serious.' I told him I was. That was over three years ago.

"I love my work. Everyone should love their work, but they don't. People get their lives into a real mess. I really like to help people straighten their lives out. Have you ever watched the show Cops? I have a couple of friends that I've always competed with. We challenge each other and demand the best from ourselves. We'll say, 'I can do that better and faster,' and then we go for it. We were watching Cops and I said, I could do that. I mean, those cops are in there being counselors, teachers, and facing the worst in people. People need to have a chance to turn their lives around.

"My friends laughed at me. I know people who have gone through junior college to get into law enforcement but I told my friends, I'm going to an elite academy, one with really advanced training. My attitude is that I can do anything I put my mind to. I applied and I was accepted. I was the oldest guy there. Those other guys were younger, faster, and in better shape. But they didn't have the life experience I have. I would speak up in class and say, that's not how it is in life. It's not the way it says in the books. Then I would say to the instructor, you should know that! Anyway, after a couple of weeks I didn't know if I could make it. I wasn't in the physical shape that these younger guys were in. I really had to stop and reframe my thinking to get back on track. I did, and I recently graduated from the academy."

I had been listening, entranced, to Greg's stories. Now he said, "Hey, come on up and see the stars." I entered the darkened room and marveled at the magical night sky. Greg picked up a pointer and began going around the room pointing out various constellations and stars. He was knowledgeable and enthusiastic and enjoying himself. So was I. When he finished he said he wanted to add a little color to a couple of falling stars and nebula and then he would be done. "You know," he said, "no one else does these stars like this. You're getting a great sky." Somehow, when Greg says it, it doesn't seem to come from his ego. It seems to come from his satisfaction at having challenged himself to do his best. "It's not about money, you know," he muses. "Other people who do this work get mad because I do more and don't charge more."

I think what a good husband and father this man would be and I ask if he is married or has children. He's married he tells me, but he doesn't have kids yet. "I'm still building my empire," he reflected, "and kids require time. Parents don't give kids the time and guidance they need to grow up and really succeed in life. If I have kids I want to really be there for them."

In awhile Greg packed up his equipment and came down. "Go up there tonight and then call me and tell me if you like it." The stars had looked great when he showed them to me with the windows darkened earlier but I was excited to go up that evening and just sit quietly, reveling in the night sky by myself. I had turned the black light on a few minutes earlier to get the stars glowing and when I turned the light out they sparkled brightly. They were different than when he had showed me earlier. I walked around the room, delighted with the subtle colors he had added – greens and blues and oranges – that gave movement and texture to falling stars, galaxies, comets and nebula. And such brilliant stars. This little cupola, with it's beautiful views by day, had turned into a mesmerizing work of art at night – an artistic replica of the night sky that is, as Greg said on his way out, going to be there forever.

I looked at the business card he left and it was perfect. A caricature of a man in a suit and tie with a wand, waving stars into the night sky. And as beautiful as the stars that will remain, I know I will sometimes pause to remember the unique star man

- and wonder what adventures he has embarked upon and what lives he has touched. I was also left with a wonderful reminder: We all have the potential to wave our magic wands and become a positive influence in the world. We just need to tap into the quiet space of our own creative minds and then put our inspirations into action.

Logic and cold reason are poor weapons to fight fear and distrust. Only faith and generosity can overcome them. - Jawaharlal Nehru

What is needed, rather than running away or controlling or suppressing or any other resistance, is understanding fear; that means watch it, learn about it, come directly into contact with it. We are to learn about fear, not how to escape from it. - Krishnamurti

When you have come to the edge of all the light you know and are about to step off into the darkness of the unknown, faith is knowing one of two things will happen: There will be something solid to stand on or you will be taught how to fly. - Edward Teller

It is cynicism and fear that freezes life; it is faith that thaws it out, releases it, sets it free. - Harry E. Fosdick

No passion so effectively robs the mind of all its powers of acting and reasoning as fear. – Edmund Burke

Your greatest gift lies beyond the door named fear. – Sufi saying

Faith in yourself and faith in God are the key to the mastery of fear. – Harold Sherman

So called "positive thinking" is no weapon against fear. Only positive faith can rout the black menace of fear and give life a radiance. – Marion Hilliard

To leap across an abyss, one is better served by faith than doubt. – Amar Jyoti

Faith begins as an experiment and ends as an experience. – W. R. Inge

Fear knocked at the door. Faith answered. – Irish proverb

Let nothing disturb you. Let nothing frighten you. Everything passes away except God. Teresa of Avila

A little faith brings your soul to heaven, but a lot of faith will bring heaven to your soul. – Dwight L. Moody

Faith is an invisible and invincible magnet, and attracts to itself whatever it fervently desires and calmly and persistently expects. – Ralph W. Trine

CHAPTER 9

From Fear to Faith

Faith is sometimes spoken of as "blind faith" and having faith in temporal things can be blinding, especially when colored by strong emotion. A mother's blinding love, for example, might give her faith in the innocence of her delinquent child against all evidence. But the faith we are referring to here is faith of a divine order. Although faith can't be seen or touched or known through the senses or intellect, it is a belief in something that can be perceived through an inner knowing. When you live with a primary focus on your physical relationship to the world you are subject to physical limitations. When you consciously integrate the other aspects of your being - mind and spirit - you expand your potential exponentially.

According to Gerald Jampolsky, there are only two emotions from which all others arise – love and fear. Love is the foundation of positive emotions, fear is the foundation of negative emotions. When we fear something we tend to develop an unreasonable hatred toward the feared object. So we come to hate and fear. We can see this not only on a personal level but in national and international tensions, where fears have grown into intense hatreds. These hatreds not only hurt us psychologically and spiritually and aggravate world tensions – but such negative concentration tends to attract the very things that we fear.

Love, on the other hand, is transformational. Cultural beliefs sometimes breed fear about other cultures, yet if we get to know individuals from different cultures or countries or religions, we find that our likenesses are much greater than our differences. Mother Teresa was a living example of the transformational nature of compassion. She embraced the unknown with love and faith – which is to say, with fearlessness. As an amazing example, she once crossed a bridge to a town under siege, despite being stopped by soldiers before crossing and warned of the dangers. She didn't take sides, only patients. She walked into the town unharmed and tended to all.

When fear is over something unknown one way to overcome it is to get acquainted with the thing that we fear. We can begin to do that by educating ourselves. Prejudice can come from this kind of fear. If we want to overcome our prejudices, we can become acquainted with the people or ideas we are afraid of.

A woman named Helen had such a fear of a certain ethnic group of people. Then her husband got transferred to a town where she found herself living amongst these people whom she had always feared. Because she was a musician, a friend suggested that she get acquainted with the music of these people. The same friend introduced Helen to a woman about her own age, with two children the same age as her children. As soon as the children met they ran off together and the women began to get acquainted. Eventually each of them attended the other's church together and they became fast friends.

Very often practical measures can be undertaken to overcome our fears. If we are afraid of things like natural disasters – tornadoes or earthquakes – we can learn the safety rules. When a fear is over something like heights we can use desensitization techniques in hypnosis, which can often lead to very effective and rapid change. Most of us have known people who are afraid of mice or snakes or even dogs, all of which can benefit from these techniques.

A less common but interesting story, is about a woman who was afraid of cats. Not wild cats or mountain lions, but common, ordinary house cats. Every time this woman saw a cat she screamed and became hysterical. She had the idea that every cat she encountered was going to leap at her throat. So a wise friend said to her, "You need to get acquainted with a cat!" But the woman adamantly refused. "Are you afraid of a kitten?" the friend asked. And she wasn't, as long as it was small enough. So the friend showed her a cute little kitten and asked her if she was afraid of it. "Not that little thing!" she responded. She was loaned the kitten to feed and play with. Of course the kitten grew into a cat but by then the woman had gradually gotten desensitized and was too attached to it to give it up.

In other kinds of situations we may be confronted with difficult circumstances in which the most powerful thing we can do is put ourselves into the higher hands of faith. Peace Pilgrim defined faith as "a belief in something that can't be perceived through your senses or understood with your intellect - but can be perceived through an inner knowing. To me, faith represents that people can, through their own free will, reach out and contact God, and grace represents that God is always reaching toward people."

I had such an experience during a personal retreat in Hawaii. Each day I would go out in the early morning and walk for miles along beautiful sandy beaches. One early morning as I walked along a remote dirt road toward a quiet beach I saw three large men walking toward me in the distance. Their loud voices carried in the breeze and my stomach caught in a knot when I realized that they were talking about molesting me. I am a fairly small woman and I knew I couldn't outrun them. There didn't seem to be any way out of this horrifying situation. Then words that I'd heard my dear friend, Peace Pilgrim, speak when she had talked about defending a young girl came to my mind: "I knew she was in great danger because of her fear."

Immediately I visualized lifting the fear up out of my body and I noted that the tension began to dissipate. Then I visualized lifting the three men and myself into God's hands. As I surrendered to the situation, knowing that it was out of my control, I felt a sense of calmness run through me. When the men were close enough I made eye contact with each of them and in the cheeriest voice I could muster in the situation, I greeted them with "Good morning!" The three scary men suddenly looked like school boys as their eyes dropped to the ground and they stumbled over their feet, mumbling "Good morning" in response.

I was totally taken by surprise, never anticipating that I would walk away from that situation unharmed. "No one walks more safely than one who walks humbly and lovingly," Peace's voice echoed, "for they shall reach the good in the other person and the person will be disarmed." It was a powerful demonstration of the reality that faith casts out fear, and in addition there was this bonus: when we face difficulties with love and faith, the obstacle in our path may simply disappear.

One cannot help but be in awe when he contemplates the mysteries of eternity, of life, of the marvelous structure of reality. It is enough if one tries merely to comprehend a little of this mystery every day. - Albert Einstein

Nothing in all Nature is more certain than the fact that no single thing or event can stand alone. It is attached to all that has gone before it, and it will remain attached to all that will follow it. It was born of some cause, and so it must be followed by some effect in an endless chain. - Julian P. Johnson

The law, "Whatsoever a man sows that he shall also reap," is inscribed in flaming letters upon the portal of Eternity, and none can deny it, none can cheat it, none can escape it. - James Allen

A grain thrown into good ground brings forth fruit; a principle thrown into a good mind brings forth fruit. Everything is created and conducted by the same Master: the root, the branch, the fruits – the principles, the consequences. - Blaise Pascal

No ray of sunlight is ever lost, but the green which it wakes into existence needs time to sprout, and it is not always granted to the sower to live to see the harvest. All work that is worth anything is done in faith. - Albert Schweitzer

People make the mistake of identifying themselves with their body, then if something happens to a person's body, they think something has happened to the person. When you think about it, that's as ridiculous as saying that if something happens to the clothing I'm wearing, something has happened to me. Our body is just what we wear. We need to take care of it, but it's not who we are. - H. Frederick Vogt

Our birth is but a sleep and a forgetting: The soul that rises with us, our life's star, hath had elsewhere its setting, and cometh from afar; Not in entire forgetfulness. - William Wadsworth

In our quiet moments, when we are not relating to traditional thinking patterns, we are certain of our own immortality and of the promise life holds for us. We know that we did not begin at conception, and that we will not end when the body is no longer able to serve our needs. - Roy E. Davis

CHAPTER 10

Understanding The Big Picture

When we take the perspective of the big picture we begin to see that everything happens for a reason. We are personally and collectively being given opportunities to learn and grow from the challenges that come our way. We can't always know the reason or see the big picture or feel the Great Spirit behind everything, but it is there nonetheless. That is the foundation of faith that great mystics and spiritual teachers have realized from within. These spiritual principles, we are told, do not only apply sometimes to some people, but to all of us all of the time.

How can such principles apply to the terrible situations we see in the world, to atrocities like the holocaust or the horrors of "ethnic cleansing" that still occur or even the violence within our own culture? From the limited perspective of personality and ego it would seem impossible and it is from here that people cry out in despair, "How can God allow these things to happen?" It is only when we step back and see from a bigger perspective that a sense of understanding or peace can come. The universe is constantly unfolding in compassion and is abundant in grace and blessings, but because of free will we often close ourselves off by neglecting to honor those higher laws. Instead we attempt to appease our hurts through hate, greed and retaliation.

The biggest lessons confronting humankind continue to include the rationalization that in some cases we can justify killing fellow human beings, and that it's okay and even desirable to attempt to grab more than our share of the worlds material goods. It is a struggle toward maturity that takes place between the ego or childlike part of our nature that sees itself as the center of the universe (either individually or as part of a larger group), and the higher nature, which sees itself from the perspective that we are a part of the whole. In our immaturity we believe that violence justifies violence, or that the end justifies the means. In our growing maturity we have the opportunity to understand that only a good influence can overcome an evil one, and that the means ultimately determines the end.

Many individuals and nations find it hard to recognize and accept the universal law that nonviolence is the only real solution to violence. It has been demonstrated many times by those who have had the maturity and insight to try it. World War II, unlike unpopular wars such as Viet Nam and the Iraq War, was a time in which many people felt that violence was not only an acceptable response, but the only effective deterrent. In spite of that popular belief, many heroic and transformational stories surfaced of facing the violence and hatred of that time with non-violence and compassion.

The Danish people, for example, heard that German soldiers occupying France were sometimes killed by the French as they patrolled neighborhoods and that then the Germans would wipe out entire blocks in retaliation. When soldiers marched into Denmark the Danes began a program of non-cooperation. Following the example of their king, Danish people protected the Jewish population by donning the arm bands that were intended to identify and separate the Jews. Danish citizens also began to approach patrolling soldiers, telling them that as Nazi soldiers they had no right to be there, any more than Danes would have a right to be in Germany. But as young men far away from home they were probably lonely and if they would put their guns aside they were welcome to come into their homes to share an evening meal. That got many of the German soldiers thinking about what they were doing there. The Danes earned great respect among the young German soldiers and in acts of conscience, great numbers of them serving in Denmark deserted from the army.

In this case it was the inspiration of the Danish king who led the people to an incredible demonstration of higher principles in action. We certainly live in times that call for truly heroic examples and perhaps it is the people who will influence the "kings" if enough of us get together for that. As Mahatma Gandhi once said,

"You may never know what results come from your action. But if you do nothing, there will be no results."

George Ritchie, author of Return From Tomorrow, told an inspiring story that took place when he was a medic in the army in 1945. He was sent into Germany to give medical help to prisoners who were being liberated from concentration camps. One of the camp inmates had been given the nickname Wild Bill because of his resemblance to the old western hero. Wild Bill was working with the American soldiers because he knew several languages and was a good interpreter. At the end of long days the American soldiers would be tired and ready to quit but Bill pressed on. "This old man has been waiting a long time. Let's take him," he would say.

Ritchie assumed that Wild Bill had only recently been incarcerated because unlike the others, his eyes were bright, he stood tall and straight and he wasn't emaciated. He was exceptional in many respects. Despite the fact that hatred among different nationalities in the camps sometimes ran almost as deep as hatred against the Nazis, Wild Bill was respected by everyone. When Ritchie saw Wild Bill's papers he was amazed to find that he'd been there since 1939. "For six years he had lived on the same starvation diet, slept in the same airless and disease ridden barracks as everyone else, but without the least physical or mental deterioration."

Feelings against Germans ran so strongly in the camps that some of the liberated prisoners had already gone into nearby towns with guns to shoot Germans on sight. The Americans were working to try and prevent the shootings and Wild Bill worked with them, talking to the different groups and enjoining them to practice forgiveness.

Talking to Wild Bill one day, Ritchie said, "It's not easy for them to forgive. So many of them have lost members of their families." Wild Bill then told his own story for the first time: "We lived in the Jewish section of Warsaw - my wife, our two daughters and our three little boys. When the Germans reached our street they lined everyone against a wall and opened up with machine guns. I begged to be allowed to die with my family, but because I spoke German they put me in a work group. I had to decide right then, whether to let myself hate the soldiers who had done this. It was an easy decision, really. I was a lawyer. In my practice I had seen too often what hate could do to people's minds and bodies. Hate had just killed the six people who mattered most to me in the world. I decided then that I would spend the rest of my life - whether it was a few days or many years - loving every person I came in contact with."

Even in the face of the destruction of his beloved family, Wild Bill was able to retain a big picture perspective. He refused to succumb to the hate that had killed the people he loved most in the world and he refused to become a victim. Many things happen in life that we cannot explain in terms of the life we are living or the perception of our five senses. It is the perception of something bigger, a spiritual foundation, that compels us to long for meaning and purpose even amidst unthinkable destruction. We can't control what happens in a given moment but we can control our response to it. In many ways, it is the great traumas that teach us and grow us more deeply if we are willing to stay the course.

There are times, especially after having experienced a major breakthrough or understanding, that it may feel as if all our problems have been solved. We've seen the light and now all is well. In reality, each giant step forward is preparing us for the next leg of the journey. Challenges are part of our experience at every stage because it is through solving our problems that we learn and grow, and it is trust and faith that sustain us through these times.

When we look at the world from the perspective of our five senses we strive for power or advantage. We may sometimes talk of an afterlife but we don't really believe. When we look from the perspective of the bigger picture we can realize that we take what we are with us, including the consequences of the choices we've made. Everything we do matters – starting with the thoughts we choose and the actions that follow. When we realize this, our choices become very different.

II know of no more encouraging fact than the unquestionable ability of man to elevate his life by conscious endeavor. - Thoreau

We're like tea bags: We don't know our strength until we get into hot water. – Bruce Laingen

One of the secrets of life is making stepping stones out of stumbling blocks. – Jack Penn

You can measure your own worth by your reactions to adversity. – J. M. Jussawalla

Adversity may call out dormant powers that have never before been suspected. – Alice H. Rice

Adversity has the effect of eliciting talents which in prosperous times would have lain dormant. – Horace

Comfort and prosperity have never enriched the world as much as adversity has. Out of pain and problems have come the sweetest songs, and the most gripping stories. – Billy Graham

Bad times have a scientific value. These are occasions a good learner would not miss. – Ralph W. Emerson

Out of clutter, find simplicity. From discord, find harmony. In the middle of difficulty, lies opportunity. – Albert Einstein

It may serve as a comfort to us, in all our calamities and afflictions, that he who loses anything and gets wisdom by it is a gainer by the loss. – Roger L'Estrange

The ultimate measure of a man is not where he stands in moments of comfort and convenience, but where he stands at times of challenge and controversy. – Martin L. King, Jr.

The gem cannot be polished without friction, nor man perfected without trials. - Chinese proverb

Most of our obstacles would melt away if, instead of cowering before them, we should make up our minds to walk boldly through them. - Orison Swett Marden

Although the world is full of suffering, it is full also of the overcoming of it. - Helen Keller

CHAPTER 11

When Bad Things Don't Get Better

Not all of what we call "bad things" go away. We can be born with permanent or long term disability, an accident or illness can cause irreversible damage, a loved one can die. We can't change the circumstances of these things, but we can change or heal on psychological and emotional levels. This is where we maintain power over our attitudes and response to difficult challenges in life.

In the natural order of things there is a tendency or push toward harmony and balance. The more out of balance we become the more painful the effects. Pain, whether physical or emotional, is a great motivator to push us back in the direction of balance, and balance always comes from taking the higher path. The higher path is the one that is based on the highest principles and integrity, not only for our personal good but for the good of the whole. It isn't always an easy path but it is the one that will lead to a state of inner peace. We aren't responsible for the things that are out of our control, we're only responsible for those things that we can control – our own attitudes and responses to a given situation.

A positive attitude is realistic rather than Pollyannaish. There is no "happily ever after" in the sense that if we achieve that one big goal in life – we find our perfect mate, or we land that job we spent ten years training for, or we win that million dollar lottery - we will never suffer or be faced with a great challenge. Challenges are grist for the mill, the fuel that forces change and growth. From that perspective we can begin to realize that problems serve a purpose. Without them we wouldn't grow.

What is it that we're growing toward as we face the challenges that life provides? We're growing toward strength and maturity, toward stable states of inner strength and joyfulness that can accompany us even during the difficult outer times. We're growing toward empowering and healing attitudes that will enable us to meet life's challenges with courage and fortitude. The attitudes we choose have everything to do with how we perceive the events in our lives and the joy or frustration of our days.

The vast majority of the time, things tend to go right whether we notice it or not. If we set reasonable goals there is a good chance that we can find the means to make them happen. Sometimes, even if something doesn't seem possible, we can find the means to make it happen if we're willing to suspend our disbelief. This natural tendency toward balance and harmony is so pervasive that the overwhelming inclination toward success tends to be taken for granted. But what if we put all of our good effort into something and things still don't work out. Does that mean we have failed? Even when things appear not to be working, what we learn from the experience in time and retrospect can be a valuable lesson or gift.

These principles are not a simple treatise on positive thinking. Of course positive thinking is a powerful step, the first step even, but positive thinking in itself is not enough. All the positive thinking in the world is not going to solve our personal or collective problems without belief and action. Positive thoughts, then, prepare us to move into belief followed by action. If we think we can, we will act and may find that we can. If we think we can't, in all likelihood we won't even try. If we do try it will be with the outcome of failure in mind, which we will probably achieve.

When bad things don't get better we sometimes need to step back and recognize that we don't always see the whole picture. What we're left with is the current reality of a given situation. What is, is. A terrible accident could leave us paralyzed. The kind of personal growth that can come out of such an extreme difficulty is what has enabled individuals like Christopher Reeves to be an incredible inspiration to so many others. He has shown us what is possible with fortitude and courage. Or Helen Keller, who said, "I thank God for my handicaps, for through them, I have found myself, my work and my God."

The atrocities inflicted during times of war are a classic example of situations in which we feel we have no control, and yet out of these most desperate circumstances have come proof that as human beings we are ultimately in charge of our own attitudes and, within limits of individual endowment and environment, we choose our own way. As one of the utmost authorities in the world, having survived a Nazi death camp in which he witnessed first hand the extremes of behavior with his fellow inmates, Victor Frankl wrote, "Man has both potentialities within himself: which one is actualized depends on decisions but not on conditions." His first hand experience convinced him that human beings have a freedom of will which cannot be taken away even when all other freedoms are stripped away. When all else is gone, we still choose the attitude toward which we will meet those circumstances.

Frankl described the conditions of camp life - the lack of sleep due in part to the vermin infested and over-crowded barracks, the lack of even minimal hygiene and sanitation, the insufficient food and the utter mental degradation. "In the final analysis it becomes clear that the sort of person the prisoner became was the result of an inner decision, and not the result of camp influences alone. Fundamentally, therefore, any man can, even under such circumstances, decide what shall become of him - mentally and spiritually. He may retain his human dignity even in a concentration camp."

Most of us are not given the task of facing such a harsh physical and emotional environment. During difficult times we can usually look, at least in part, at our belief around a particular situation or condition. A disempowering belief will postpone healing. (I'll never get over this pain/disappointment/shame.) An empowering belief will hasten our healing. (I can't change what has already happened, but I'll find a way to move on.) Can we influence the outcome? Absolutely. Every moment we influence everything around us with our thoughts. Mind affects matter just as physical laws do. What we dwell upon we increase.

When we only look at the surface of things we may miss the workings of cause and effect, which is the natural tendency of all things to move toward harmony and balance. It sometimes requires stepping back and looking from an objective or big picture perspective. When we make good and responsible choices we are giving ourselves every opportunity to improve our conditions and circumstances – and most especially, we are creating a healthy mental and spiritual state.

Never lose an opportunity of seeing anything that is beautiful; for beauty is God's handwriting – a wayside sacrament. Welcome it in every fair face, in every fair sky, in every fair flower, and thank God for it as a cup of blessing. – Ralph W. Emerson

Your divine nature – a drop of God – can be awakened when you touch a truth from outside, so that it confirms that truth. Or the truth can come directly from the inside. Have an inspirational time and fill your life with inspirational things to awaken your divine nature. – Peace Pilgrim

The thing which we speak of as beauty does not have to be sought in distant lands. It is here about us or it is nowhere. – Allen Tucker

Nature is painting for us, day after day, pictures of infinite beauty if only we have the eyes to see them. – John Ruskin

If I were to name the three most precious resources of life, I would say books, friends and nature; and the greatest of these, at least the most constant and always at hand, is nature. – John Burroughs

The art of being happy lies in the power of extracting happiness from common things. - Henry Ward Beecher

The best and most beautiful things in the world cannot be seen or even touched. They must be felt within the heart. –Helen Keller

When you are inspired by some great purpose, some extraordinary project, all your thoughts break their bonds; your mind transcends limitations, your consciousness expands in every direction, and you find yourself in a new, great and wonderful world. Dormant forces, faculties and talents become alive, and you discover yourself to be a greater person by far than you ever dreamed yourself to be. - Patanjali.

Love is the flower of life, and blossoms unexpectedly and without law, and must be plucked where it is found, and enjoyed for the brief hour of its duration. -D.H.Lawrence

Live your life each day as you would climb a mountain. An occasional glance toward the summit keeps the goal in mind, but many beautiful scenes are to be observed from each new vantage point. – Harold V. Melchert

CHAPTER 12

Surround Yourself With Inspirational Things

Innspirational things lift us up and connect us with our higher nature. Peace Pilgrim said, "Your higher nature is a drop in the ocean of God – and has access to the ocean." Sometimes we access our higher nature through the inspiration of beautiful music or surroundings. Such occasions may bring up insights, glimpses of universal truth, or connect us with a sense of inner guidance. We can also connect with our higher nature through beautiful written or spoken words, when we feel an inner sense of confirmation. Or as Peace says, "You can directly perceive truth from the inside. All inspired writing came from the inner source, and you too, can receive from that source."

Inspiration is a state of mind and mind is something that we have direct influence over. We can slip into states of mind that can become a habit. We may, for example, develop a habit of worry or a habit of positive expectation. We always have a choice in the matter, though we may not be aware that we are making that choice. The key is awareness. Before we can make changes we need first become aware of what it is that we are changing or aspiring toward.

You can access the healing power of inspiration by taking your focus inside, in a quiet state of meditation or self-hypnosis. Use your imagination to create an inner sanctuary – a place that inspires you and lifts you up. Your inner sanctuary is a very personal space.

It might be abstract, like glowing color and flowing sound; it might be an incredible garden or place in nature that you've actually seen or simply imagine; or you might imagine a special room filled with everything you love. You can bring in as many senses as possible – sight, sound, touch, even taste and aromas. The more senses you call on the more real and inspiring it becomes. A fascinating aspect of using imagination is that the subconscious mind doesn't distinguish between what is real and what is imagined. Therefore our bodies respond with the same pleasurable and healing energy we would experience if we were actually in the setting we are vividly imagining. This is also an aspect of visualization that makes it an effective technique for creating the changes you want to move toward in life.

Another way to create inspiration is in a journal. You can use a personal journal to record beautiful thoughts, prayers or poetry; you can create collages of things that inspire you – art, photos of nature or beautiful landscapes or gardens or homes or any of the things that fuel your passion. Creating this kind of journal can provide an uplifting reprieve in difficult times or the peace of respite in a quiet moment, a place to reconnect with the things that fuel you through the adventures and challenges of life.

You can also create your external environment, your home, yard, garden, office or work space, to be places that inspire and lift you up. Everything in your environment has a subtle effect on you, adding to your comfort and ease or discomfort, your peace and serenity or tension. You can pay attention to color, cleanliness, clutter, objects that elicit emotional triggers, functionality, esthetic beauty. Look around your office or a particular room in your home. What inspires you or calms you? What stirs your emotions – positively or negatively? What is the room primarily used for, and what is the feeling you want to experience here? You will probably want to feel creatively inspired in a room that is used as an office or art studio, or perhaps the kitchen, where food can be creatively prepared. In a workout or game room you probably want to be inspired to rev-up your metabolism and move. In a bedroom you want to elicit feelings of relaxation and calmness.

In addition to creating an inspirational setting in your home and office, it's beneficial and healthy to go to inspiring places such as spending time in the beauty of nature. It can be healing for mind, body and spirit to bicycle in the park, walk on the beach, go sailing, camping, hiking, skiing or whatever outdoor activities you enjoy. From Japan there is a concept called "forest bathing" in which it's considered healing for the immune system to breathe in phytoncides, which is a substance emitted by plants and trees and generally means the aroma of the forest. Results are said to last up to a month. The Forest Therapy Association of the Americas states, "The therapeutic benefits of forest bathing may be difficult to fully explain with only phytoncides, but most likely, the green scenery, soothing sounds of streams and waterfalls, and natural aromas of wood, plants and flowers in these complex ecosystems all play a part."

Sometimes we become so used to our environment that we stop "seeing" what is there. We stop noticing how we feel when we enter a certain room but many objects reflect a particular energy. For instance, a woman who had been divorced for more than two years was asked by a feng shui expert what she felt when she walked into her bedroom. The bedroom was filled with massive, dark, expensive looking furniture. "Well, I think at least I got something good out of a lousy marriage." The furniture was a constant reminder of a painful situation, but she hadn't looked at it from that perspective. Incidentally, that same woman had been hoping to find a new relationship but hadn't been getting anywhere. Her feng shui guide suggested she get rid of the furniture and replace it with something that reflected herself, which she did. Soon afterwards she entered a new relationship. Perhaps after removing the trigger for all those negative feelings she was more emotionally open and ready to move on.

Peace Pilgrim, a woman who counseled others in healing their lives and also in physical healing had this to say about inspiration: "I wish for all a complete healing - not through the suppression of symptoms by drugs, but through the removal of cause. I hope you will be inspired to put yourself on a really excellent health diet. I hope you will be inspired to search for and remove all negative thoughts and feelings. I hope you will be inspired to fill your life with beautiful things - the beauty of nature, uplifting music, beautiful words and meaningful activities. Stay away from everything that pulls you down, and stick to the things that lift you up!"

Focusing on the positive and surrounding yourself with things that lift you up is a choice. You make it every day. The wonderful thing about focusing on the positive is that once you've broken a habit of negative focus, your positive focus becomes habit. What you focus on you tend to bring into manifestation. When you surround yourself with inspiration you are working on healing all aspects of yourself - physical, as well as mental, emotional and spiritual.

Whenever we bemoan our destiny on Earth and complain of our ill-fortune, we are railing against our own choice - not the choice of some arbitrary god or gods who have done us a bad turn. – Stewert C. Easton

God impels nobody, for He will have no one saved by compulsion. God has given free will to men that they may choose for themselves, either the good or the bad. – Hans Denck

Nature gives man corn but he must grind it; God gives man a will, but he must make the right choices. – Fulton J. Sheen

There are two freedoms: the false, where a man is free to do what he likes; the true, where a man is free to do what he ought. – Charles Kingsley

Mankind's greatest gift, also its greatest curse, is that we have free choice. We can make our choices built from love or from fear. - Elisabeth Kubler-Ross

We cannot lead a choiceless life. Every day, every moment, every second, there is a choice. If it were not so, we would not be individuals. – Ernest Holmes

By choosing we learn to be responsible. By paying the price of our choices we learn to make better choices. – Marsha Sinetar

The strongest principle of growth lies in the human choice. – George Eliot

Destiny is not a matter of chance, it is a matter of choice; it is not a thing to be waited for, it is a thing to be achieved. – William J. Bryan

The highest knowledge which man can attain is the longing for peace, that our will becomes one with the infinite Will. – Albert Schweitzer

You choose yourself to be a receiver of spiritual truth when you surrender your will to God's will. We all have the same potential. God is revealed to all who seek – God speaks to all who will listen. When you surrender your will to God's will you enter a very busy life – and a very beautiful one. – Peace Pilgrim

CHAPTER 13

Free Will

We live in a world in which there is free will. What does that mean? It means that everything we do is a choice, even when we think we aren't choosing. When we were children our parents would say, "Clean up your room and finish your homework." It seemed like we didn't have a choice, but we did. We could not clean our room and not do our homework - and suffer the consequences. Maybe you tried that. If you didn't like the consequences you might have then decided to go along with the parental direction. That's how we learn to distinguish between choices that get us what we want or need, and choices that prove we have free will and don't have to listen to anyone, even if we suffer for it. If suffering (for no good reason as opposed to for a good cause) makes us feel powerful, we may still be using that tactic.

Life is a series of choices and we constantly use our free will to make those choices. When we begin to make good choices of our own free will, choices to be of service, to be responsible, to live with integrity, then good things come in greater abundance, including good feelings and insights.

So often we hear people blaming God for some tragedy or the loss of a loved one. Why did God take my (husband, wife, child, etc.). Look at all the innocent people who get killed in the commission of a crime or who become "collateral damage" during wars. Is God really the one who is taking our loved ones, the innocent victims of crime and war or illness or accidents? Of course not. In our hurt and anger and rage we sometimes look for someone or something to blame. It's time to bring that responsibility closer to home.

Some things are easier to understand. In war for example, both sides may pray to God and both sides may generally think they are in the right. Does God choose sides? Does God sanction the building of bombs and bullets, or the training of human beings to hate and kill each other? Or do people? Of course people do. And then people die, even innocent people caught in the middle. Children. We call the people who do the killing on the other side enemies or terrorists. Perspective comes from whichever side we're on. It is we human beings who carry the responsibility.

An innocent person gets killed during the commission of a crime. A human being is responsible. In addition to that, society is responsible. We make choices about what is appropriate and acceptable. This is our free will. We do it individually and collectively. We allow guns to be manufactured and sold. We say it is our right to own and bear arms. We can say we have been victimized and we have - by our choices. On some level we can understand that God is not responsible for the choices made by human beings with free will.

Illness can be more difficult to understand, especially when children are affected or even born with painful or chronic conditions. Beautiful, sweet, innocent children we say, and they are. And they are often courageous and loving beyond words. Where is free will, we might ask. It is not with the rational mind that we will find the answers or understanding to comprehend the seemingly incomprehensible. It is only when we look from the highest place within ourselves – our own higher nature – that we connect with an infinite wisdom and know that spirit reaches beyond the earth life and beyond any currently existing circumstances. The beautiful, innocent ones teach us so much about our own capacity to love and sacrifice for others. Perhaps their struggles are a gift that they chose to bring with them, a pathway to opening our hearts and compassion and appreciation for the preciousness of life.

No matter what you are confronted with, or how seemingly insurmountable a difficulty might seem, it is through free will – your own choice, whether consciously or unconsciously conceived – that you choose the role you will play. You can be a victim and curse fate or the powers that be, or you can be empowered and confront whatever difficulties come your way with perseverance and compassion.

Many spiritual teachers have called the universe a school and said that we're here to learn lessons. It is possible to step back and look at life from this broader perspective and even to gain appreciation for the challenges that test us in the relatively short time period we are given - short, and not always predictable. From this perspective you can also learn to give thanks and appreciation for all of the opportunities you are given to express and receive love and forgiveness, and for your free will to make choices as to how you will spend the time that is given to you. Whenever you make a choice to let go of anger and victimization, you are stepping away from a crushing burden to a place of empowerment. This is both a free will choice and a freeing choice.

Life has taught me that it knows better plans than we can imagine, so I try to submerge my own desires...into a calm willingness to accept what comes. - Julia Seton

When we are true to an ideal, we can trust Life to deliver to us because we are doing what we should do. This cures every sense of fear and worry. - Dan Custer

Life is like that, one stitch at a time, taken patiently, and the pattern will come out all right, like the embroidery. – Oliver W. Holmes

Life goes on – never the same – but onward, spiraling, expanding, and growing – always an adventure. – Margaret Pounders

Life is a gift from God, an unlimited series of opportunities to find the good in ourselves and others. – Alan Cohen

The sun shines after every storm; there is a solution for every problem, and the soul's highest duty is to be of good cheer. - Ralph Waldo Emerson

I like living. I have sometimes been wildly, despairingly, acutely miserable, racked with sorrow, but through it all I still know quite certainly that just to be alive is a grand thing. - Agatha Christie

Our way is not soft grass, it's a mountain path with lots of rocks. But it goes upward, forward, toward the sun. - Ruth Westheimer

To sit patiently with a yearning that has not yet been fulfilled, and to trust that that fulfillment will come, is quite possibly one of the most powerful "magic skills" that human beings are capable of. - Elizabeth Gilbert

For a long time it had seemed to me that life was about to begin – real life. But there was always some obstacle in the way, something to be got through first, some unfinished business, time still to be served, a debt to be paid. At last it dawned on me that those obstacles were my life. – Alfred D'souza

Life is a great school for the development of character, and all through strife and struggle, vice and virtue, success and failure, we are slowly but surely learning the lessons of wisdom. – James Allen

CHAPTER 14

Trust Life to Bring You What You Need

Empowering attitudes and beliefs are the foundation for creating the life you want to live. They are a requirement for trusting life. To be empowered or have positive attitudes may at first seem like an attempt to gain more control, but trusting life means accepting that we don't always have control. We don't see the big picture or know why it is that difficulties come our way. When challenging things happen we can choose to feel like a victim, depleting our creative motivation, or we can choose the belief that there is a higher order. Nothing happens randomly and whatever comes our way has something valuable to offer us: It might teach us something or give us an opportunity to be of service. When life gives us lemons, we can make lemonade.

It isn't that once you accept a positive focus everything becomes easy. In truth, it can be very difficult to find direction or to keep centered and focused in the midst of difficult circumstances. But the more you open yourself to trusting universal principles and accept that the things that come serve a purpose - perhaps teach you something - the more you begin to build confidence in their workings. It may be tempting to dig in and resist challenges when they come, or try to muscle your way through to a rigidly defined outcome. Valuable lessons can be learned that way, although usually with more energy and frustration.

As an example, when I (Randal) was 26 I found a charming redwood cabin on an acre of land next to a stream. When I arrived, it was love at first sight. The location just outside of city limits was perfect, with a driveway that wound down through thick trees, offering me the seclusion and lovely natural setting and wildlife that I cherish. The landlord warned me it was a temporary rental as the property was for sale, and that I might have only six months. I decided to rent it anyway and hoped to be able to live there for at least a year.

Over the next few years I was told several times that my notice was imminent, but I was enjoying my beloved home while it lasted and it kept turning out I could stay a while longer. I wanted to buy it, but the property was being sold as part of a group of five parcels on six acres in a prime location to be developed. The parcels finally got bought by the owner of some adjacent parcels. He planned to develop his now-expanded nine acres of parcels and I was given notice. Inexplicably, days later, the new landlord relented and said I could stay temporarily. Time passed and after this middle-aged landlord had an untimely death his son and heir put all of the parcels up for sale again. A developer planned a shopping center there that got through all the permits and seemed to be a done deal, but fell through.

The land sold to another developer, and in order to close the deal the landlord's son and heir was required to give me 30 days notice and have me vacate the property. By this time I had lived on and loved this property for 20 years! My desire was to stay if at all possible and I pursued that goal with everything I had. I repeatedly offered to buy the parcel that included my house from the developer. No deal. When I had given up hope of staying permanently and owning the parcel, I did everything I could to prolong my occupancy. I offered to be a caretaker of all the parcels for a period until the development got more imminent. No deal. Because a substantial part of my business was located on the property, I knew I somehow needed to find and move right into a permanent residence to save the tremendous work it would take to move my household and business of 20 years twice. I had very particular ideas of what I wanted, and was determined to nail it. Even though I'd paid first and last month's rent, I gave another rent check and pleaded for an extra 30 days. The 30 days notice remained firm in spite of my rent check being accepted, and it seemed an impossible mission. Escrow alone might need to be 30 days, and I had to first find the right property while working 60-hour weeks, then make an offer, and work out an agreement to enter escrow.

While working long hours and trying to negotiate with both the developer and the landlord, I spent every spare minute looking for a suitable house. My requirements included several features that were important to me: A unique, well-maintained custom country home that was close to town, in a beautiful, natural and secluded setting, included office as well as living space, and had a little acreage. The situation seemed impossible, but I decided to trust life and trust the experience. I got the necessary financial records in order so that I could apply for a pre-approved loan. I reviewed ads daily in the paper, looked at the real estate channel on TV, and drove up and down every country road surrounding the three towns I wanted to live near. (This was during the early days of internet, a few years before Google, and the web wasn't yet helpful.) There were lots of possibilities, but nothing that met all of my particular requirements.

With time running out I met with a legal consultant and it turned out my determination to be ultra-conscientious as a tenant turned out to be a life-saver in a surprising way. Having originally paid first and last month's rent, when I had given the landlord another rent check and the check was cashed, it invalidated the 30 day notice! I now had precious extra time to scramble to meet the new deadline.

By now I had turned to an established realtor. Every afternoon I would squeeze in an hour or so to meet with him and rush through a handful of selected properties for sale. And then I found it. The multi-level "treehouse" on half an acre, nestled up a slope at the end of a long driveway. The property was surrounded by trees. The home had an office on the entry level with a deck overlooking the trees, decks off the main floor that also looked into the trees, and an office and bedroom with yet another deck downstairs. Every level had a clear view to the deer that sometimes wandered through.

After just one quick dreamy-eyed look I made an offer and started negotiations. Incredibly, everything came into place just in the nick of time. At midnight on the day I was required to leave my rental house I moved out the last of my belongings and took possession of my new home. In retrospect it was one of the times is my life that I was most aware that life can be trusted to bring us what we need.

Discernment allows us to see something through vision that isn't colored by emotion. It is something that develops through our consistent efforts to understand and apply higher principles to our lives. One of the things that discernment can teach us is how to be proactive in a way that is in harmony with the forces at play rather than against them. Another characteristic of discernment is non-attachment to outcomes. Attachment to an outcome engages our emotions and leads us to apply principles of the rational mind, which can cancel out intuition or higher guidance. The following story illustrates the principle of non-attachment:

I (Cheryl) decided I was ready to buy a house, and maybe there is something in that relationship to a home, a place of respite and security, that lends itself well to understanding this principle of trusting life. Valuable insight can often be gained by looking in retrospect at the experiences in our lives.

While vacationing near one of my favorite places in nature, Yosemite, I found a little community that immediately felt like home. It was an answer to the question I had been posing – where do I want to live? I felt a feeling of rightness about this decision. For the next year and a half I spent my free time looking around the area, getting acquainted and looking at houses that were for sale. Every time I went the area seemed more right to me but that special house hadn't shown up. When it did show up it was out of my price range. I attempted to creatively negotiate a deal but the offer wasn't accepted. Someone else got the house.

I was disappointed but not discouraged. Another house came up that seemed perfect and this time the offer was accepted. When the house went into escrow a home inspection uncovered serious problems. I decided to let it go. Now I was beginning to feel discouraged. I had expended a lot time and effort in the pursuit of the "right" house and nothing seemed to be working. I was about to give up but unexpectedly woke up one morning with a strong urge to drive up to that area and look around one more time.

While talking to my parents on the phone I blurted out without forethought, I'm going to find my house today! Then I shrugged off the impulsive comment, intending to just enjoy the day. I arranged to see some houses through a local realtor. One house in particular seemed very interesting. The price had just been lowered but it was still out of my range. I decided to look at it anyway and fell in love with it. I called it the cathedral chalet, placed in a thicket of pines with a magnificent giant oak tree that shaded the house and part of the large wrap-around deck. I knew it was out the question so I just admired it.

The realtor called a week later to say that the price had just dropped another ten percent, and the sellers were very motivated. It was still out of my range but I couldn't resist another look. It was a nice fantasy that could be enjoyed for a little longer. "The owners have said to bring in any offer," the realtor encouraged me when I came to look at it again. I hesitated, then asked the realtor if she would mind bringing in a really low offer. "Can't hurt," the realtor laughed. "We'll give it a try." To both of our surprise, the owners countered by accepting the price but as is.

The house was wonderful but seventeen years old. I told the realtor it was a fantastic deal but the house was a bit of a fixer and I wouldn't have the extra capital if any major repairs were needed. The realtor suggested that I have a house inspection, saying the deal could always be negotiated more. I agreed, figuring again that I could keep the fantasy for a little longer.

Sure enough, the house inspection showed costly repairs to the roof and deck. I told the realtor I couldn't afford the repairs and asked her to convey to the owners that it was a great deal and I really appreciated it, even though I couldn't afford to go through with it. Then I was scheduled to go out of the country for several days. In my mind I just let it go. When I returned the realtor called to say that the owners were anxious to be in touch with me and had agreed to my offer - and that they would pay for the repairs. There wasn't anything I could do to get out of this house deal. It just kept pursuing me!

We are confronted all the time with great lessons, and we always have a choice. We can attach ourselves to outcomes, we can let our emotions bring us into mood swings or negative expectations and thinking, or we can learn to trust life. We can let go of our tight hold on the reins and know that opportunities are all around. If one thing doesn't work out, the next is just around the corner.

The same is true of the tragedies that come our way. Life includes birth and death, grief and celebration, sadness and joy. It is a potpourri of experiences that we can meet head on, learn from and transcend. Underlying everything is the solid foundation of spirit. We can trust life to unfold. And we can trust ourselves to deal with what comes.

Non-judgmental justice flows naturally from understanding the soul and how it evolves...the continual incarnation and reincarnation of the energy of the soul into physical reality for the purpose of healing and balancing its energy in accordance with the law of karma. – Gary Zukav

Man is the sole and absolute master of his own fate forever. What he has sown in the times of his ignorance, he must inevitably reap; but when he attains enlightenment, it is for him to sow what he chooses and reap accordingly. – Geraldine Coster

Cause and effect, means and ends, seed and fruit, cannot be severed; for the effect already blooms in the cause, the end pre-exists in the means, the fruit in the seed...You cannot do wrong without suffering wrong. - Ralph W. Emerson

A human being fashions his consequences as surely as he fashions his goods or his dwelling. Nothing that he says, thinks, or does is without consequences. - Norman Cousins

In this world everything changes except good deeds and bad deeds; these follow you as the shadows follow the body. – Ruth Benedict

Not in the heavens above, nor in the farthest reaches of the sea, nor by transporting yourself to the remotest valleys of the mountains, will you be able to hide from the consequences of your own evil actions. Likewise, certain are the blessings growing out of your good actions. – Buddha

We sow our thoughts and we reap our actions; we sow our actions and we reap our habits; we sow our habits and we reap our characters; we sow our characters and we reap our destiny. – C. A. Hall

Life is a perpetual instruction in cause and effect. - Ralph Waldo Emerson

Through the law of cause and effect we choose our destiny. Moreover, we are our own prophets for we constantly project our future state by the seeds we plant in the present. - Cheryl Canfield

CHAPTER 15

Cause and Effect

The law of cause and effect is also called karma: As you sow so shall you reap, which may be seen not only in the pattern of a lifetime but over a span of many lifetimes. When the world is viewed from the concept that there is no afterlife or that this life is all there is, what becomes valued are the things that can be gained in this life, such as power and possessions. Or we may speak of a belief in an afterlife without accepting the possibility of a series of lives, in which a life is like a day in our evolution. Our choices might be very different if we looked at this life as but one small part of a larger whole, in which the decisions and choices we make affect not only this life, but lifetimes to come.

Looking at life from this perspective we could even say that through the law of cause and effect we are molding our destiny. In a sense we are our own prophets because with every thought and action we are planting the seeds of our future. When we plant seeds of positive thought and follow through with constructive action we move toward a positive outcome. The opposite is also true. This law of cause and effect is like planting a garden. We can seed flowers of positive thought or weeds of negativity. Either way, the seeds are watered by our passion and action. What isn't watered withers. There are no shortcuts in the garden of our lives - we reap the bounty of what we sow through our own efforts.

These natural laws, based on principles of harmony, can be seen to exist as guidelines to human conduct. To the degree that they are recognized and lived in accord with, they move an individual or a society toward survival and stability. When they are disregarded, they move an individual or society toward disintegration and destruction. Natural laws have to do with compassion, equality, sharing, integrity, fairness, truth, oneness, and so on. Rather than religious concepts natural laws can be viewed as self-evident, validated by experience. When we live these principles they are reflected back to us. When we live with dispassion, prejudice, greed, deceit, unfairness and falsehood, we reap what we sow. If we want to change our experience we can change the seeds of our thoughts and actions.

We can find examples of self-evidence in the experiences of life. A child eats too much candy at Easter time or Halloween - and goes to bed with a stomachache. A person smokes two packs of cigarettes a day for thirty years and gets lung cancer. These relationships are easy to see. It is more difficult to see the relationship between discordant choices and consequences which haven't shown up yet. Most of us have heard of someone who has smoked for years or who exists on junk food "and has hardly ever been sick in his/her life!"

But what if we are responsible for every thought, word and action in our lives, not only in this lifetime, but until we learn the lessons of compassion and balance that lead to stability and harmony? What if we could step into the big picture and see ourselves in a subsequent life, born in a weakened body linked to the unhealthy habits of our previous life? Or as the very kind of person we were prejudiced against in a past life? A person of color, someone plagued with obesity or hunger, a despised sexual orientation, or a particular gender we have deprecated? What if the injustice we perceive in this limited life view is really unplayed out karma, a result of cause and effect, and everyone will be held accountable for every thought, word and action not only in this lifetime, but until individually and collectively, we learn the lessons of compassion and non-judgment?

Imagine what kind of world we might live in if this perspective were adopted globally. All of the injustices we perceive from our limited view of life would be changed. We could see the birth of a soul as an evolutionary process, already full of experiences and perceptions and personality. All souls being equal but at varied stages of growth – and with free will to advance or coast or retreat in any given period. We might be born more or less gifted or handicapped by the circumstances and heredity of our births. A courageous soul may have taken on great challenges in order to learn and teach others. A timid soul may take on very few challenges. We may not know why we came in with the gift of musical genius or so poor that as children we often went to bed hungry. But we could accept that even though we don't see the whole picture, our lives are the playing out of a larger evolution of our souls on their journey toward wholeness.

Gary Zukav has described an individual life as an episode in that soul's journey, each with an epitaph at the end: To be continued. Not only each life or each day, but each moment is an opportunity to create anew - our thoughts, our beliefs and our actions. The universe reflects our beliefs back to us. When we think in terms of victim consciousness we will continue to attract the kind of energy we are projecting. Not only do negative thoughts attract like energy, but negative beliefs attract their own confirmation. As James Allen stated, "As a man thinks in his heart, so is he."

Through the law of cause and effect we choose our destiny, for we constantly project our future state by the seeds we plant in the present. In our shortsightedness we sometimes think that what we do in the present is not important in certain circumstances, even though we know that it is bad for us. In some situations our poor choices are even supported by loved ones or authority figures.

A man named Bill, for example, was dying of cancer. Bill was a chain smoker and an alcoholic. The cancer had spread throughout his emaciated body, and he got around in an electric wheel chair. "Smoke and drink all you want," his doctor had sympathized. "It doesn't really matter any more." But of course it did. It always matters. The state of our consciousness at death is the consciousness we take right over with us.

Bill was miserable and almost everything he said came from an attitude of feeling sorry for himself. Then his long estranged daughter found out where he was and wrote him a loving letter. She wanted to see him. He could hardly believe it. Her letter touched him deeply and he wanted to see her more than anything, but in his condition he was too ashamed. Then he did something that took a lot of strength and courage. He stopped smoking and drinking so that he could face his daughter. It was a great reunion in which Bill discovered that it wasn't too late to feel good about himself. He died shortly thereafter, having made peace with at least some of his demons.

These ideas, of course, have been around for centuries and are part of many philosophical and religious understandings. Peace Pilgrim, who's story is highlighted in the next chapter, had this to say: "Some problems that are brought over with you are karmic - subject to the law of cause and effect. You might say you came to solve them. It is important that they be solved. That's at least one of the reasons you came. Some problems are caused in this earth life by wrong eating, or wrong thinking and feeling. They might be caused by eating junk food, or thinking junk thoughts, like hate thoughts. While tendencies toward certain difficulties can be inherited, remember you choose the conditions of your birth." And we choose the conditions of our lives every day – through our thoughts and actions. We have it within our own mind and heart to create and live lives of meaning and purpose.

This is the way of peace - overcome evil with good, falsehood with truth, and hatred with love. The Golden Rule would do equally well. These are laws governing human conduct, which apply as rigidly as the law of gravity. - Peace Pilgrim

Everything you do should be done with peace. That is the best medicine for your body, mind, and soul. It is the most wonderful way to live. - Paramahansa Yogananda

Each one has to find his peace from within. And peace to be real must be unaffected by outside circumstances. – Mohandas Gandhi

Peace lies not in the external world. It lies within one's own soul. – Ralph W. Trine

Our work for peace must begin within the private world of each of us. – Dag Hammarskjold

Whoever lives in the spirit lives in perennial peace. - Paul Brunton

Your own self is your ultimate teacher. The outer teacher is merely a milestone. It is your inner teacher that will walk with you to the goal, for he is the goal. - Nisargadatta

There can never be peace between nations until there is first known that true peace which...is within the souls of men. – Black Elk

I like to believe that people in the long run are going to do more to promote peace than are governments. Indeed, I think that people want peace so much that one of these days governments had better get out of their way and let them have it. - Dwight D. Eisenhower, 1959

The search for inner peace is the search for our natural self, where we touch the essence of life itself. A place where we are wise, joyful, vibrantly alive—we are who we are meant to be, whole and holy, at peace, in peace, radiating peace. This is where all is possible and everything begins. - Louise Diamond

If we have no peace, it is because we have forgotten that we belong to each other. - Mother Teresa

CHAPTER 16

Peace Pilgrim: *Teachings of a Modern Mystic*

In the summer of 1952, a woman named Mildred Norman set out to hike the entire length of the 2,050 mile Appalachian Trail. She was the first woman to accomplish this feat in one season, which turned out to be a trial run for the journey she was about to begin. In 1953, alone and without the support of any organization or group, Mildred took the name Peace Pilgrim and started out on a pilgrimage for peace that lasted until her death over 28 years later.

What is as amazing as her ongoing journey is the time in history in which a lone woman had the courage to set out on foot to open minds and hearts. The war in Korea was raging and the McCarthy era was at its height. Congressional committees considered people guilty until proven innocent and as a result there was much fear. The safest thing to be was apathetic, and yet a small middle-aged woman decided to call herself Peace Pilgrim and step forth to wake people up from their apathy and get them thinking.

From the beginning Peace understood that by living in accordance with those universal laws of peace and harmony everything would work out. With simple faith she followed the guidance of that "still small voice" inside. On January 1, 1953 she stepped out at the head of the Rose Bowl Parade in Pasadena, California. She was dressed completely in navy blue - pants, shirt, tennis shoes and a tunic with pockets all around the bottom that contained all she owned: a comb, a toothbrush, a pen and small leaflets that she was passing out. She chose the color blue because she considered it symbolic of peace. White letters across the front of her self-designed tunic read PEACE PILGRIM and on the back, WALKING COAST TO COAST FOR PEACE. She didn't carry money and she didn't accept any.

As she walked along ahead of the march a policeman approached from behind and touched her shoulder. "Oh, oh," she thought. "I'm about to be moved off the line of the march." But instead the policeman wished her well and said, "There ought to be more people like you."

Peace saw a truce in Korea that first year and continued walking through the unrest of the sixties. In 1964, eleven years after the start of her walk, the message on the back of her tunic changed to 25,000 MILES ON FOOT FOR PEACE, and after that she stopped counting. She continued walking through the difficult days of Vietnam, into the seventies, and until her death in 1981.

You might wonder what kind of background Peace came from to step into such an unusual and dedicated calling. Her roots were quite modest. She was born in 1908 and grew up on a farm in New Jersey, and there was little to suggest in her early life that she would become a wandering sage dedicated to inspiring people to work for peace both in the world and in themselves.

As a little girl of three Mildred could recite long poems, without even knowing what all the words meant. As she grew she continued to have an exceptional memory. She taught herself to play the piano over the course of one summer and was a very bright student. She had the highest grade point average in her senior high school class.

Her family was very peace oriented, having come to this country to escape militarism in Germany, but they weren't religious in the traditional sense. "My first view inside a church was when I was twelve years old and I looked through the doorway of a Catholic church to watch janitors clean the cathedral. When I was sixteen I entered a church for the first time to attend a wedding." With no formal religious training, Mildred set out to do her own investigations about God.

In a history class she came across the Golden Rule in a text that compared this universal idea as it ran through many religions and it struck her as truth. As a senior in high school she began asking everyone she thought might know, "What is God?" But she never got an answer that satisfied her. Then when she was out on a long walk with her dog, she found her own answers. "Intellectually I touched God many times as truth and emotionally I touched God as love. I touched God as goodness. I touched God as kindness. It came to me that God is a creative force, a motivating power, an over-all intelligence, an ever-present, all pervading spirit - which binds everything in the universe together and gives life to everything."

But this insight was not the turning point of her life. After high school she found a job and enjoyed spending her money on nice clothes and a fancy car. She had a busy social life, wrote and directed plays, and married a handsome young man with whom she had little in common. It was a difficult marriage that ended in divorce. It was at this time, unhappy and questioning her way of life, that Mildred had what she referred to as a religious experience:

"I became increasingly uncomfortable about having so much while so many people in the world were starving. I had to find another way... In desperation, and out of a very deep seeking for a meaningful way of life, I walked all one night through the woods. I came to a moonlit glade and prayed. I felt a complete willingness, without any reservations, to give my life - to dedicate my life - to service. 'Please use me,' I prayed to God. And a great peace came over me."

Mildred spent the next fifteen years preparing for her pilgrimage, although she didn't know at that time what she was preparing for. Her life became more and more simplified until she had reduced her wardrobe to two dresses and was living on ten dollars a week. It was a time when she struggled between what she called the lower self and the higher self. "The body, mind and emotions are instruments which can be used by either the self-centered nature or the God-centered nature. The self-centered nature uses these instruments, yet it is never fully able to control them, so there is a constant struggle. They can only be fully controlled by the God-centered nature. When the God-centered nature takes over, you have found inner peace...."

It was after having found this inner peace that Peace was ready to step out as a pilgrim and share the steps that had led her to this point. She walked in complete fearlessness, facing a near-death experience in a snowstorm, skeptical interviewers, a rough individual in the desert – all in the first year. She was even picked up by FBI Agents as she walked along the highway, somewhere between El Paso and Dallas. She was counting the miles she walked so before getting into the car she scratched a large "X" in the dirt so she could return to that same spot to continue. She was taken to prison and booked for vagrancy:

"They first take you in for fingerprinting. I was fascinated because I never had fingerprints taken before – or since! He then took a chemical and, just like that, he got all the black ink off my fingers.

"I spoke to him as I would speak to anybody I was with, and something very interesting happened. Apparently he was used to being treated in a very uncooperative manner. When I treated him like a human being he gave me a lecture on fingerprinting and he showed me the charts. I had really not learned that much about fingerprinting before. People were waiting, but I didn't know that until I came out of the room and saw the long line.

"Then they took me in to be photographed and hung a number around my neck with a chain. When they were photographing me from the front and side, I remembered all those pictures of wanted people you see in the post office. I remembered how mad they all looked, and I said to myself, 'Let me be different.' And I smiled as sweetly as I could. There's one smiling face somewhere in rogue's gallery!

"Then they took me in to be questioned. They actually sat me under a strong light – it's supposed to have a psychological effect on you. But I had already been on television at that time, and I said to myself, 'Do they really think that's a strong light? They should see the lights in a television studio!' At that time TV lights were not only bright but hot.

"They first asked me if I would answer any question, and I said, 'Certainly I will answer your questions. Not because you are law enforcement officers, but because you are fellow human beings, and I answer the questions of all my fellow human beings. Whatever you are in your official capacity, you are first and foremost a human being. And if we could get together as human being to human being we can get done much faster.' And it ended it up that way!

"They began with the confusing technique. One would fire a question at me. Before I could answer the other would fire a question at me. I had to keep saying, 'If you will pardon me for a moment while I answer the other

gentleman's question.' Then they got down to meaningful questions such as college students ask me. How I warmed up to the subject!

"Then they referred to physical violence as being the intent to hurt. They said, 'Would you under any circumstances use or sanction the use of physical violence?' I said, 'No, this is contrary to God's laws. I would rather have God on my side than any power on earth.' I told them the story of the disturbed teenage boy who hit me during our walk."

(Peace had gone for a walk with a teenager who was afraid that if he went by himself he might get hurt and there would be no one to help him. Everyone else was afraid to go with him because he was known to be violent. He had once beaten his mother so badly that she had to be hospitalized. He was a large young man, built like a football player, but Peace wasn't afraid. Then as they got to the top of a hill an unexpected thunder storm came along. The boy was terrified and he went crazy, going at Peace with his fists. Instead of running away she held up her arms to his blows and looked at him with the deepest compassion. The hitting soon stopped and he was terribly remorseful, saying that his mother always hit back. It was a transforming experience for him, and he was never violent again.)

"Then they said, 'Suppose it was necessary for you to defend a loved one?' I said, 'Oh, no, I do not believe I could defend a loved one by disobeying Divine Law.' I told them about the eight year-old girl who had been left in my care and the experience we had with the psychologically sick man who tried to harm her."

(Peace had been staying at a ranch and when the family went into town they asked if she could look after their eight year-old daughter. Peace was writing a letter on the porch when she saw a car drive up with a man inside. The little girl saw him also, and looked scared. The girl ran when the man got out of the car and he chased her into the barn. When Peace got to the barn the girl was cowering in a corner and the man was coming at her slowly and deliberately. Peace put her body in front of the girl and looked at the psychologically sick man with compassion. He came close and then stopped abruptly, as though he had run into a wall. He looked at them for a long while and then walked away, without ever speaking a word.)

"Suppose I had been so foolish as to forget the law of love by hitting back and relying on the jungle law of tooth and claw? Undoubtedly I

would have been beaten – perhaps to death, and possibly the little girl as well. Never underestimate the power of God's love – it transforms!

"Then they got into things very philosophical and said, 'If you had to choose between killing and being killed, which would you choose?' I answered, 'I don't think I would need to make such a choice – not as long as my life remains in harmony with God's will. Unless, of course, it was my calling to be a martyr. Now, that's a very high calling and a very rare calling. I don't believe it's my calling – but the world learns to grow through its martyrs. If I had to make a choice, I would choose to be killed rather than kill.'

"They said, 'Could you give a logical explanation for such an attitude?' Here I was, attempting to explain the attitude of the self-centered nature and the attitude of the God-centered nature so they could understand it! I told them that in my frame of reference I was not the body. I was just wearing the body. I am that which activates the body – that's the reality. If I am killed, it destroys merely the clay garment, the body. But if I kill, it injures the reality, the soul! And they put me down as having a religious basis for my pilgrimage.'"

Peace remained a wandering pilgrim throughout 28 and a half years, without ever having a home. She once said that the only day off she took every year was Christmas – because everyone else was busy.

On the second year of her pilgrimage Peace did take a sabbatical in which she fasted for 45 days. She undertook the fast as a spiritual discipline, to keep her focused on her prayer for peace. During that period she was staying at the home of a chiropractor who used fasting as a healing process in his work with patients. He wasn't treating Peace but he was interested in observing her, as he had never fasted a well person.

The last meal before Peace fasted was a grapefruit and two oranges, then for 3 days she took neither food nor water. After that she drank distilled water at room temperature for the duration of her fast. At some point during that time she had a beautiful vision that started out as a dismal cross hanging over her. She knew someone had to take the burden so she reached up to accept it and was immediately lifted above the cross, where all was light and beauty. The message she received was that all she needed was the willingness to accept the burden. In that acceptance she was lifted above it where instead of hardships, she found a wonderful sense of peace and joy. From that point on she was able to pray without ceasing – which she described as a constant projection of positive thoughts.

During her travels Peace deeply affected the lives of many individuals. On one occasion a saloon keeper called her into his tavern and offered her food, which she gratefully accepted. As she was eating he asked, "How do you feel about being in a place like this?"

"I know that all human beings are God's children," she replied. "Even when they are not acting that way I have faith that they could, and I love them for what they could be."

When Peace got up to leave she noticed a man standing by the bar with a drink in his hand. When he caught her eye he smiled a little and she smiled back at him. "You smiled at me," he said in surprise. "I should think you wouldn't even speak to me but you smiled at me." She smiled again and said, "I'm not here to judge my fellow human beings. I'm here to love and to serve." The man suddenly went to his knees at her feet and said, "Everyone else judged me, so I defended myself. You didn't judge me, so now I judge myself. I'm a no-good worthless sinner! I've been squandering my money on liquor. I've been mistreating my family. I've been going from bad to worse!" Peace placed her hand on his shoulder and said, "You're God's child and you could act that way."

The man looked at the drink in his hand in disgust and hurled it against the bar, shattering the glass. Then he looked Peace in the eyes and said, "I swear to you I'll never touch that stuff again. Never!"

Peace was able to learn the end of the story when she heard from a woman in that town a year later. She said that as far as anyone knew the man kept his promise. He had stopped drinking, gotten a good job, and was getting along well with his family. "When you approach others in judgment they will be on the defensive," Peace said. "When you are able to approach them in a kindly, loving manner, without judgment, they will tend to judge themselves and be transformed."

Cheryl met Peace at the Theosophical Society in 1975 and Peace became her beloved friend and mentor. Cheryl's time with her included accompanying her on an inspirational and educational retreat to Alaska in 1979 and to Hawaii in 1980. Peace continued walking until her death in 1981. She was killed when riding in a car on her way to a speaking engagement. A car crossed over the double line and hit the car she was in head on. Her words and stories continue to reach into our hearts:

"We must walk according to the highest light we have, encountering lovingly those who are out of harmony, and trying to inspire them to a better way. Whenever you bring harmony into any unpeaceful situation, you contribute to the cause of peace. When you do something for world peace, peace among groups, peace among individuals, or your own inner peace, you improve the total peace picture.

"Goodwill will win in the world. The darkness that we see in the world today is due to the disintegration of things that are not good. Only the things that are good can endure. Yes, love will win in this world. Those who are filled with hatred are desperately unhappy and desperately - even though unconsciously - seeking a better way. Only those who are filled with love are serene and at peace."

After Peace's death, Cheryl and four others compiled the book, *PEACE PILGRIM: Her Life and Words in Her Own Words,* which has become a spiritual classic with over 500,000 copies in print. A non-profit organization, Friends of Peace Pilgrim was formed and the book and other Peace Pilgrim materials are distributed free of charge, and are available online.

in May 2017, Peace was inducted into the New Jersey Hall of Fame. Just weeks later, she was inducted into the Appalachian Trail Hall of Fame. What began as "one little person giving all of her time to peace," grew into a world wide community of peace makers inspired by her life and message. As Peace proclaimed, "Many people, giving some of their time, can make history."

Once in a very great while we meet, whether in the flesh or on the screen or in written story, an individual whose life deeply touches us and has an impact that words can scarcely describe. Peace Pilgrim was such a person. She left an indelible impression because she lived her beliefs, and when your life is in sync with your beliefs, you become much more powerful.

The natural healing force within each of us is the greatest force in getting well. – Hippocrates

The last place we tend to look for healing is within ourselves. – Wayne Muller

When we begin to trust ourselves more, the body begins to renew itself and becomes healthy and filled with life energy. – Shakti Gawain

The hours of trial are the hours that make us strong. Thus hard conditions may be for you like a little bit of flint striking upon you to ignite the fire of real life. - Paramananda

Healing proceeds from the depths to the heights. – Carl Jung

We are healed from suffering only by experiencing it to the full. - Marcel Proust

Tears which have no vent in sorrow make other organs weep. – William Boyd

To heal is to touch with love that which we previously touched with fear. – Stephen Levine

The more I can love everything – the trees, the land, the water, my fellow men, women and children, and myself – the more health I am going to experience and the more of myself I am going to be. – Carl Simonton

At the deepest level, the creative process and the healing process arise from a single source. When you are an artist, you are a healer; a wordless trust of the same mystery is the foundation of your work and its integrity. - Rachel Naomi Remen

Whatever you do, if you do it sincerely, will eventually become a bridge to your wholeness, a good ship that carries you through the darkness. - Carl Jung

There are two types of healing, whether it is physical healing or otherwise. One is removal of cause, which is good. The other is removal of symptom, which merely postpones the reckoning. - Peace Pilgrim

CHAPTER 17

Cheryl's Story: *Profound Healing*

At the relatively young age of 41 I was diagnosed with advanced cancer and faced the likelihood that the life I had taken for granted would end soon. So many questions and emotions poured in. "How could this me happening to me? Why?"

What I came to discover is a process I call profound healing. Profound healing is about healing on a very deep or spiritual level which often, but not always, leads to physical healing. It comes with a penetrating sense of inner peace and a knowing that everything is going to be all right. No matter what happened, I knew I could count on inner resources to see myself through.

More than just physical wellness, profound healing can relate to any part of our lives – emotional, physical, relationships with ourselves or others, livelihood, etc. It is a deep inner healing that opens the pathway to transformation. Transformation is about moving beyond form; about bringing our lives into a place of integrity. It is a transformation from fear or anxiety to a sense of rightness about and acceptance of ourselves and our lives, no matter what the external circumstances might be.

My diagnosis of advanced cancer came more than 28 years ago. At that time I was told I might not live another six months, or be here for the birth of the child my daughter was pregnant with. Every year since then has been a milestone. Not just as a marker of my physical recovery, but as a reminder of how precious life is.

It's so easy to get caught up in the busy-ness of life, or the chaos or challenges that come our way, that we can lose sight of our unique purpose – something I believe we all have. Yet something like a life threatening illness or serious personal problem can push our focus and priorities into a much clearer perspective.

We are all born with amazing potential, which sometimes barely gets touched. That potential includes the mind/body connection as well as our potential for transformation on a spiritual level.

When I was first diagnosed with cancer the oncologist felt that my only chance for survival was a very radical surgery. He described the delicate process that would be followed by many repair surgeries throughout my life, as well as resulting in impaired bodily functions. When he finished he looked at me and said, "You look overwhelmed." I answered that I didn't think I wanted to live in the body that would be left. What I didn't tell him was that when he was describing the procedure I had a spontaneous vision of myself dead on the operating table. I chose to follow my intuition and turned down conventional medical treatments.

I am not suggesting that conventional treatment is unwarranted. What I discovered is the importance of following intuition, that internal "yes" or "no" sense that in the midst of big challenges can be very keen if we remain open to receiving it. Intuition is not an emotional or fear response, but a very clear inner knowing. It can be tempting to allow fear or the opinions of others, especially authority figures, to influence our choices, and so we drown out the voice of our inner guidance.

Trusting that inner guidance helped me gain the strength I needed to pursue my unique path. That path included both the practical and spiritual aspects of coping with a life-threatening illness. I understood and accepted the probability that I would die prematurely, but I also knew it wasn't inevitable. Life is both fragile and tenacious. I was prepared to do all I could and to leave the rest in higher hands.

My very dear friend and mentor Peace Pilgrim once said, "If we realized how powerful our thoughts are we'd never think a negative thought." This is an essential point in making that mind/body connection. Fear thoughts - or negative thoughts - gobble up our life energy, while positive and inspiring thoughts energize us. As soon as we accept the idea that we do have control over our thoughts and we can create an empowered belief system, we can replace disempowered thoughts with positive ones. Whenever we recognize a negative belief we can change it by changing our thought. We uproot the negative ones and supplant them with positive ones.

Until the time of my diagnosis I had thought I was doing things "right." I ate a healthy vegetarian diet, had a regular yoga practice, meditated, exercised. I even had a retreat center where I was teaching others to live healthy, balanced lives.

"How could this be happening to me?" I asked in my initial attempts to understand. But I soon realized it wasn't a productive question. Rarely, while in the midst of something, do we have the insight to grasp why it is happening. It is in retrospect that we can look back to see what it is we've learned or gained.

Recognizing that I could change my perspective from "Why me?" to, "If me, why?" allowed me to make empowered choices as to how I wanted to respond to this challenge. Since I considered myself to be a teacher and I was now about to experience death, I accepted this new assignment - to teach what I was learning. "How do we learn to die well?" I asked. The answer that came surprised me: by learning how to live well in the present moment. No one knows with certainty what a particular outcome will be and the present moment is really the only moment we have.

The first thing I worked on was stabilizing my body and building up my immune system. I researched alternatives, toured clinics in Mexico, and then designed a treatment plan that felt right for me. On the practical side it included diet, juicing, herbs, large doses of vitamin C, laetrile, lots of rest, and exercise. When my research uncovered the fact that cancer doesn't grow in oxygen, and I had a type of cancer that tended to metastasize to the lungs, I took up jogging. I was weak at first but I walk-jogged and built my strength and endurance.

I was also reading a lot about the power of visualization in the treatment of cancer. Most of the articles and books I found described cancer in war terms – being at war with the cancer and fighting the enemy. The idea of being at war with my body didn't set well with me but I wanted to give it a try. I attempted to use the kinds of imagery described but it left me feeling drained. After a couple of attempts I gave it up.

Then one day in my own quiet meditation/self-hypnosis I had a spontaneous image of my cancer cells as frightened young children, too young to have developed reasoning minds. In the image, these cells were being bombarded by the ongoing stress I had been experiencing in my life. In a misguided effort to survive they had begun reproducing like crazy, not realizing that in so doing their efforts would kill the host, my body, and ultimately themselves.

I was profoundly struck by the image. I immediately visualized going inside to gather up the cancer cells. I embraced them as I would young, frightened children, assuring them that they were no longer alone or helpless. They could stop reproducing. I was in charge now and I would take care of them.

I felt an instant response as a feeling of peacefulness spread throughout my body. I didn't know if I would live or die, but I knew that on a spiritual level I had experienced a profound sense of healing. The powerful impact of that experience came from my personal resonance with the image – which came from my own subconscious mind - and fit very well into my belief system.

Of course we all know we will die some day. We expect to be old, to be ready even. But I was barely into my forties. I felt as though I was just beginning to know myself. Our lives are what we measure things by. They are the totality of our five physical senses. And therein, I discovered, was the key to regaining balance and perspective under such difficult circumstances. The best I could do was choose to live consciously and lovingly, in sync with my inner sense of what was right for myself and my loved ones. That meant taking responsibility for - responding to and following - my inner direction. It was an intuitive sense that existed outside of and in addition to the five physical senses. It made its way to the foreground of my awareness and tapped me into a far deeper knowing.

This knowing is a connection to the bigger "I," an ongoing energy or force that activates the body, exists before birth into this life, and continues to exist beyond the time frame of our present personality. It was this broader perspective that enabled me to accept the situation and deal with it in faith, receptive to the great lessons coming my way.

Forgiveness, of course, is essential to being at peace and I had plenty of that to work on. I knew that the lingering resentments I felt did me no good, and neither did feelings of guilt for mistakes I had made. However, I discovered that it's one thing to want to do something, and another to actually accomplish it. So I began to practice forgiveness. Using my journal, I wrote letters to everyone I could think of that I had any bad feelings toward. Not with the intention of sending them, but as an outlet to get all that energy out that had been bottled up inside. I used those letters to express anything I had ever held back or wished I had said or done. When I finished a letter I would imagine being the person receiving it. Then I would answer the letter from the other person's perspective. Giving myself the opportunity to be the other person began to alter my perspective. I continued writing between myself and the other person until I found closure - either mutual forgiveness or an agreement to let go and move on. I did this exercise with everyone I could think of that I felt even the slightest resentment or anger toward.

This process worked well until I came to a recent wound. Even though I wanted to, I couldn't get past my feelings of resentment. No matter how many times I wrote back and forth I still felt hurt and angry. So I went to the "letters to God" section in my journal. This was a place I turned to when I felt blocked or unable to decide what to do with something. This time I wrote to God - asking God to forgive this particular person in my name until I was ready. I accepted that I was willing, but I wasn't able yet to do it on my own. I immediately felt relieved of the burden, and in a short period of time realized that my attachment to those old feelings had dissolved.

Forgiving myself was perhaps even more difficult. I wasn't always sure what it was I felt guilty about and I pondered over it. I got out my journal and wrote about it. I noted all of my imperfections. I struggled through tears, feelings of worthlessness, wanting to be somebody else. But I persevered. In the end I got to the other side where I found someone I truly liked - myself. I began to realize what it really means to love ourselves - not narcissistically, but for the courage and honesty it takes to see ourselves as we truly are and to have the same compassion for ourselves that we extend to others.

When I was able to release all that negative energy I began to heal from the inside out. Most of us aren't consciously aware of the big picture, but we can feel and experience an inner awareness of our connection to something bigger than ourselves. My experience taught me that death is not to be feared. We will all die at some point and letting go of the timing frees our energy to work on healing. The kind of healing this refers to is not always physical healing, but that profound healing that frees us to continue our soul's journey whether we heal and go on in this life or heal and pass on to the other side. Love heals and takes us wherever we need to go.

Cheryl Canfield's whole story is told in her book, *Profound Healing: The Power of Acceptance on the Path to Wellness,* which includes 12 self-help practices. Now more than 28 years since her diagnosis, Cheryl lives in Northern California where she is a Wellness Counselor and Clinical Hypnotherapist, and a primary instructor at the Hypnotherapy Training Institute in Corte Madera, CA.

At the height of laughter, the universe is flung into a kaleidoscope of new possibilities. – Jean Houston

The most wasted of all days is one without laughter. - E. E. Cumming

Sometimes I think the surest sign that intelligent life exists elsewhere in the universe is that none of it has tried to contact us. - Bill Watterson

Don't worry about the world coming to an end today. It's already tomorrow in Australia. - Charles Schultz

An atheist is a man who has no invisible means of support. - Archbishop Fulton J. Sheen

Be careful about reading health books. You may die of a misprint. – Mark Twain

Live in such a way that you would not be ashamed to sell your parrot to the town gossip. - Will Rogers

The human race has one really effective weapon, and that is laughter. - Mark Twain

I have lived with several Zen masters – all of them cats. - Eckhart Tolle

The sound of laughter is like the vaulted dome of a temple of happiness. – Milan Kundera

What soap is to the body, laughter is to the soul. – Yiddish proverb

Time spent laughing is time spent with the gods. – Japanese proverb

Laughter lifts us over high ridges and lights up dark valleys in a way that makes life so much easier. It is a priceless gem, a gift of release and healing direct from Heaven. – Alan Cohen

The greatest prayer you could ever pray would be to laugh every day. For when you do, it elevates the vibratory frequency within your being such that you could heal your entire body. – Ramtha

CHAPTER 18

The Healing Power of Laughter

Laughter has long been recognized for its power to lift the spirits and to have a positive impact on physical and emotional conditions. An astute French surgeon, Henri de Mondeville (1260–1320), wrote, "Let the surgeon take care to regulate the whole regiment of the patient's life for joy and happiness, allowing his relatives and special friends to cheer him, and by having someone to tell him jokes." But it wasn't until Norman Cousins published an article in the New England Journal of Medicine in 1976 that extensive research began.

Cousins had been diagnosed in 1964 with ankylosing spondylitis, an illness that causes inflammation of the spine and other areas of the body. The connective tissue in his spine was deteriorating and he was given a grim prognosis: He was told that he would likely live only a few months and the odds of his recovery were one in five hundred. After doing some research Cousins found that his condition tended to deplete vitamin C - so he asked his doctor, who was also his friend, to take him off of all drugs and inject massive doses of vitamin C.

Then Cousins left the hospital and checked into a motel. Reasoning that if negative thoughts and attitudes can result in illness, positive thoughts and attitudes should have the opposite effect, he rented a movie projector and a supply of funny films that included Candid Camera and the Marx Brothers. He was delighted to discover that ten minutes of belly laughter gave him at least two hours of pain-free sleep. He was also monitoring his blood sedimentation rate - a measure of inflammation and infection, and he found it dropped at least 5 points after each film watched. He followed this routine of laughter until he recovered. The article that had been printed in the New England Journal of Medicine in 1976 became the first chapter of his book, Anatomy of an Illness, published in 1979.

Since that time medical studies have shown that laughter increases endorphins, the body's natural painkillers, and suppresses epinephrine, a stress hormone. It has been called "a tranquilizer with no side effects." Professor Lee Berk, who studied the effects of laughter, has said that laughter increases the activity of natural killer cells that destroy viruses and tumors. It also increases the disease fighting B-cells and the immune boosting T-cells.

Some years ago I (Cheryl) had a personal experience of the power of laughter to take away pain and promote healing. I had come home after a long workday looking forward to a hot bath but the flame in the old water heater on my enclosed back porch was out. I was especially tired and anxious to take a bath and went out to re-light the pilot. I turned the gas on but the phone rang before I could get it re-lit. The lighting was dim on the back porch when I returned just a minute later and without thinking I struck a match in order to see more clearly. I watched in what seemed like slow motion as the inside of the heater exploded and the flames shot out, following the gas to the match in my right hand and engulfing it in a fireball before putting it out.

Feeling calm and no doubt in shock, I went into the kitchen to examine my hand. Three fingers had turned white and were hard like cardboard. There was no sensation at all. I turned on the faucet to run cool water over my hand while I closed my eyes and visualized cool water running through the inside of my hand into my fingers. After several minutes I placed my hand into a large glass of cool water and went to the bathroom to check out my face in the mirror. The hair on one of my eyebrows and one cheek had been singed off and some hair on that side of my head, but otherwise my face was undamaged. It felt good to be quiet so I sat down, keeping my hand in the water and continuing to visualize coolness flowing through the inside.

Some time later the phone rang and it was Randal. I told him what had happened and he asked if I would like him to come over and keep me company for awhile. My hand was starting to hurt and I accepted his offer, looking forward to the distraction. As we sat talking he noticed my face starting to flinch from the pain I was now feeing, and he spontaneously told me a silly joke. It struck me in a belly laughing way and then I looked at him in surprise. The pain in my hand had stopped. He started to tell me another joke but I said, "Wait! Don't tell me another one until the pain starts again!" Each time my face would begin to flinch he would tell another joke and the laughter would temporarily erase the pain. When he ran out of jokes he asked if I'd ever heard about the silly face contest and he made an outrageous face. I went into gales of laughter that sent my pain away for a long time.

As we sat there laughing I told him I was having a wonderful time and not only that, I was glad for the accident because I'd learned something very important first hand - that laughter is a great anesthesia. I went directly to bed after a hearty laugh and to sleep as quickly as possible. I was barely aware of any sensation in my hand that night. When I woke up in the morning I was surprised to find that my fingers were pink and the skin soft. There was a slight stiffness at first but no blisters, and the only effect from the burn was some slight cracking of my skin a few days later.

A big belly laugh creates a positive internal response – "feel good" hormones get released, the immune system gets an energy boost, and the hearty shaking of internal organs helps release any stress or tension built up from held-in emotions. Laughter isn't just fun, it's essential to our biological and emotional health.

Other benefits of laughter include a lowering of blood pressure, reduced stress, increased relaxation, increased oxygen resulting in more energy, alleviation of depression, a clearer mind, and an immeasurable increase in social attractiveness and enjoyment of life. The message is clear: to live better, healthier and happier - laugh more.

What lies before us and what lies behind us are small matters compared to what lies within us. And when we bring what is within out into the world, miracles happen. - Henry David Thoreau

If we could see the miracle of a single flower clearly, our whole life would change. - Buddha

It is the commonest of mistakes to consider that the limit of our power of perception is also the limit of all there is to perceive. - C.W. Leadbeater

Miracles only work through your own faith. Where there is no faith there can be no miracle. – Papa Ramdas

The man who does not believe in miracles surely makes it certain that he will never partake in one. – William Blake

To me every hour of the light and dark is a miracle, every cubic inch of space is a miracle. – Walt Whitman

Where there is great love there are always miracles. Miracles rest not so much upon faces or voice or healing power coming to us from afar off, but in our own perceptions being finer. – Willa Cather

This world, after all our science and sciences, is still a miracle; wonderful, magical and more, to whosoever will think of it. – Thomas Carlyle

I have learned, as a rule of thumb, never to ask whether you can do something. Say, instead, that you are doing it. Then fasten your seat belt. The most remarkable things follow. - Julia Cameron

According to Vedanta, there are only two symptoms of enlightenment. The first symptom is that you stop worrying. Things don't bother you anymore. You become light-hearted and full of joy. The second symptom is that you encounter more and more meaningful coincidences in your life, more and more synchronicities. And this accelerates to the point where you actually experience the miraculous. - Deepak Chopra

A strong positive attitude will create more miracles than any wonder drug. - Patricia Neal

CHAPTER 19

Miracles Can Happen When You Believe in Them

Albert Einstein said, "There are only two ways to live your life. One is as though nothing is a miracle. The other is as though everything is a miracle." Miracles, from that perspective, are really about perception. They are not consciously directed happenings, but rather a changing or opening of perception that allows for the reality of an invisible and unlimited force.

The miracle of healing that I (Cheryl) experienced, recovery from advanced cancer after a prognosis of possibly six months left to live, was from my perspective, the result of an inner healing. Whether physical healing takes place or not, inner healing leads to a sense of peace and acceptance, whatever the outcome might be. It is a very freeing perspective. What I learned or transformed from belief to knowing, is that laws that govern the physical world are limited. Consciousness that transcends the physical world is unlimited. Miracles, which seem to reverse physical law, are natural metaphysical occurrences.

Wayne Dyer has talked about meeting a man in Hawaii who was known as a healer. He asked, "How do you get to be a Kahuna?" and the man said, "Kahuna's are raised to have no doubt, to have a knowing. And when a knowing confronts a belief in a disease process the knowing will always triumph."

Dyer illustrated that principle with a story about his young daughter, who'd had a condition called flat warts since she was two and a half years old. These flat warts were on her face. By the age of seven they were getting worse, even though different doctors had said she would outgrow them and they would go away in a few months. While visiting a friend who was a dermatologist Dyer asked the man to look at his daughter. The dermatologist examined the little girl under big lights and said, "You've got flat warts." The little girl hated that term and told him so. She preferred to call them her bumps.

"Well," he said, "the good news is that when you get married you won't have them." But he didn't know when they would go away. He said he couldn't burn them off because it could burn her face. He also said that there was no medicine he could give her. But he told her that she had the ability within herself to be rid of them. "If you can call upon that healing capacity within you and begin to talk to these bumps in a way in which you ask them to leave, you have a much greater chance of getting rid of them faster than anything I could give you."

That night Dyer went into his daughter's room and she was under the covers with a flashlight. He went over and lifted up the blanket and asked her if everything was all right. "Shhh! I'm talking to my bumps," she told him. The next night and the third night the same thing happened. The conversation with the dermatologist had taken place on a Monday and by the following Friday every one of the little girl's bumps had disappeared for good.

"There is a stream of healing that is something we can plug into that is something like electricity," Dyer explained. "When we go into that stream of healing with a knowing we go to a higher level within ourselves and we don't allow any doubt in. In every human being there are two parts of us: The ego - earth guide only - which says that who I am is separate from you, from God, from my environment. Then there is the Sacred or Higher Self, a mystical awareness that says I'm connected. It doesn't care what you have. This is the part that wants us to be at peace, while the ego says it's more important to be right."

A clinical psychologist named Wes Hiler said, "Spiritual healings are called 'supernatural' because they are rare and we have not yet learned all the laws involved in their operation. Nor have we been able to replicate them at will. They seem to be different from events of everyday life. But life itself is a miracle; the existence of living organisms could not be anticipated on the basis of the laws of physics and chemistry. We are so accustomed to such organisms, however, that we forget the enormous complexity and ingenuity to be found in all living creatures. Therefore we do not recognize the miraculous nature of life."

What is a miracle anyway? It might be an extraordinary or awe-inspiring event that elicits an incredulous response. "What was the chance of that happening?" To those who respond to such events as random happenings, the little miracles of every day are more likely to go unnoticed. To those who respond to the synchronicity of an event with a belief in divine guidance or in the unexplained forces of nature and the universe, the experience of miracles becomes more abundant. If you don't believe it, experiment with a change of attitude and perception - and see what happens. If your expectations in life are generally low you can be pretty sure that you will meet them. Set your expectations high and you might be surprised by what you can accomplish. Here is another story to inspire you:

Luther Burbank was a pioneer who discarded the limitations of popular belief in the field of horticulture and created miracles. He devoured Charles Darwin's two-volume treatise in 1868 entitled "The Variation of Animals and Plants Under Domestication," which espoused the idea that organisms vary when they are removed from their natural conditions. Convinced that plants, as well as people, behave differently when in a different environment, he began to order varieties of plants from countries like Japan and New Zealand to cross with homegrown plants. The results included thousands of varieties over his lifetime, like the Climax Plum that tastes like pineapple, and the Royal Walnut that outgrew regular walnuts eight to one, and which Burbank hoped would revolutionize the furniture business.

When he later happened upon a seed ball in his potato field he applied Darwin's theory. Since potatoes almost never set seed they are propagated from the buds or "eyes" of the potato. He knew that when potato seeds were found they would grow a batch of hybrids and that got him excited. What if one of the hybrids developed into a miracle potato? He experimented with the 23 seeds in the ball and one of them gave him a variety that doubled the average yield. It was white and creamy, unlike the common red skinned variety. This excellent baker was purchased by a seed man and went on to dominate the US potato market.

Not miracles you say? When Burbank wanted plants to develop in some particular and new way uncommon to their species he would get on his knees and talk to them. He believed that plants have more than twenty sensory perceptions that we are unable to recognize because they are different than our own. He didn't know if they could understand his words, but he felt that they could comprehend his meaning. Burbank went on to develop a spineless cactus. "While I was conducting my experiments with cacti," he said, "I often talked to the plants to create a vibration of love. You have nothing to fear," I would tell them. "You don't need your defensive thorns. I will protect you." According to Manly P. Hall, "Burbank explained to me that in all his experimentation he took plants into his confidence, asked them to help, and assured them that he held their small lives in deepest regard and affection."

The epicenter of the earthquake that devastated San Francisco in 1906 was actually closer to Santa Rosa, which was also laid waste. Luther Burbank lived in Santa Rosa and while everything around it lay shattered and broken, not a pane of glass in Burbank's huge greenhouse was even cracked. Quietly, Burbank surmised that his communion with the forces of nature and the cosmos might well have protected his greenhouse. He believed in and accepted the miraculous in his everyday life.

To a crowd gathered expecting to hear him give explicit details on how he produced all of his horticultural wonders he said, "Preconceived notions, dogmas and all personal prejudice and bias must be laid aside. Listen patiently, quietly and reverently to the lessons, one by one, which Mother Nature has to teach, shedding light on that which was before a mystery, so that all who will, may see and know. She conveys her truths only to those who are passive and receptive. Accepting these truths as suggested, wherever they may lead, then we have the whole universe in harmony with us."

One who breaks an unjust law that conscience tells him is unjust, and who willingly accepts the penalty of imprisonment in order to arouse the conscience of the community over its injustice, is in reality expressing the highest respect for law. – Author Unknown

Each man must for himself alone decide what is right and what is wrong, which course is patriotic and which isn't. You cannot shirk this and be a man. To decide against your conviction is to be an unqualified and inexcusable traitor, both to yourself and to your country. - Mark Twain

Peace is not a relationship of nations. It is a condition of mind brought about by a serenity of soul… Lasting peace can come only to peaceful people. - Jawaharal Nehru

Deep within us all there is an amazing inner sanctuary…a holy place, a divine center, a speaking voice, to which we may continually return. Eternity is at our hearts, pressing upon our time-worn lives, warning us with intimations of an astounding destiny, calling us home to Itself to be awakened. – Thomas Kelly

There is a divine plan behind everything, and if we allow ourselves to be used by that Unseen Force, as good instruments, many things can happen in a mysterious, miraculous way. – Satchidananda

If only you will find out the thing God intends you to do, and will do it, you will find that all doors will open to you; all obstacles in your path will melt away; you will be acclaimed a brilliant success. – Emmet Fox

Every good that you do, every good that you say, every good thought you think, vibrates on and on and never ceases. The evil remains only until it is overcome by good, but the good remains forever. – Peace Pilgrim

The breeze of grace is always blowing on you. You have to open the sails and your boat will move forward. – Ramakrishna

It is one of the beautiful compensations of this life that no one can sincerely try to help another without helping himself. – Charles Warner

The supreme law of the land is the Great Spirit's law, not man's law. - Proverb

CHAPTER 20

The Spirit of the Law

In 1979 I (Cheryl) went to Alaska on an inspirational and educational tour with Peace Pilgrim. We were a group of 18 adults, living outdoors and traveling in three crowded cars. The trip was designed to give us an experience of living simply and included vegetarian fare, eating most of our meals, as well as sleeping, outdoors. The conditions of the trip were hard on some and one or two people left early on. For those who remained, it was sometimes difficult and tiring. Tempers occasionally flared. The day that we learned a lesson on the spirit of the law was one such day.

The group was in a beautiful state park and after cleaning up the dinner dishes and packing things away, someone started to question Peace about where we would spend the night. Peace pointed to a small hill a short distance away and indicated the meadow on the other side. "But there's no camping in this park," one of the men informed her. "Oh, we're not going to camp," she replied. "We won't have a fire or anything. We're just going to sleep." What followed was a life lesson I have never forgotten.

The same man who had informed Peace that camping wasn't allowed came back a short time later. "Peace," he said, "I just talked to the park ranger and asked if we could sleep here. He said we're not allowed to stay overnight." Everyone looked at Peace. "Never ask!" she scolded him gently. "If you ask, authorities are in a position of having to enforce the letter of the law. I live by the spirit of the law, always respecting where I am and leaving it better than I found it. Now that you've asked we'll have to leave."

Though the sun was still up in the summer Alaskan sky, the hour was late. Gear had to be gathered and piled into cars and we drove many miles before a place was found to pull over and sleep. The debate was hot in my car. "How could she do that! Expecting us to break the law!" I sat silently, quietly relishing the words Peace had spoken: Spirit of the law. The feel of it rolled over me like a refreshing shower.

In retrospect, I reflect that the lesson of this little incident grows continually deeper. It is so often tempting to simply follow the rules blindly in order to escape embarrassment or punishment or worse. It starts at home when small children sometimes learn to block the drive of their own growing independence for fear of the parental voice: Do as I say or... Children in heavily structured or punishing environments tend toward either rote obedience or defiance.

The same is true of society. Whenever laws or rules become too rigid or limiting, or the ability to make decisions becomes fear based, creativity and spirit get compromised or squashed. A letter of the law attitude is punitive. It results in living with a sense of apathy or unwillingness to take risks that could ostracize an individual from family or society or lead to punishment; on the other side, it leads to rebellion and defiance.

Any time that laws become so rigid and pervasive that they intrude even into the private lives of citizens, as they did during the McCarthy era, and as began again during the Bush II administration, people are in danger of falling into a dangerous state of apathy or hopelessness or despair. The scary and imaginative Orwellian fiction, "Big Brother is Watching," is a reality in the United States today. Cameras, for example, are everywhere. People who live in cities and are out and about are caught on film sometimes dozens of times in a day. Private phones are randomly tapped. Cell phones and the internet have opened up a virtual baring of our private lives and information. The result of this kind of violation of privacy and pressure to follow the letter of the law leads to a sense of disconnection or not belonging, pervasive underlying fear, automatic adherence to orders without questioning, and a stripping of our sense of individuality or creative efforts.

On the other side, the results of rigid control are defiance, gang activity, violence, substance abuse, escalating criminal behavior, over-populated prisons, and extreme prison sentences for minor crimes.

The perspective of the spirit of the law can bring refreshing solace. Not to be abused or used as an excuse to do whatever one pleases, certainly not an excuse to break the law or to exploit others or the environment; the spirit of the law enables us to honor the intention of given rules and laws that are meant to be just and serve the whole, rather than blind obedience. It enables us to maintain our integrity, our creativity, and the courage to do what we feel from our own knowing is right in challenging circumstances, regardless of the consequences. This is the motivation behind such movements as conscientious objection, which has taken place throughout history as individuals follow the call of their conscience in declaring that they will not take up arms against fellow human beings during wars - often choosing to serve in civil or medical capacities, or even jail sentences when alternative service is denied.

As we look back at history we can often see how great leaders are born out of times of unjust laws that exploit or target certain groups or populations. Mohandas Gandhi, a revered leader of his time, created a movement he called Satyagraha, meaning soul force or truth force, that can be seen as an international lesson in applying the spirit of the greater universal law of fairness and justice. He used civil disobedience to break what his conscience considered to be unjust laws, with the willingness to accept the penalty - which in some cases led to physical beatings and at other times, imprisonment. He first led a campaign against anti-Indian legislation in South Africa in 1906, and continued perfecting his Satyagraha methods when he returned to India several years later.

In India, the British government held a monopoly on mining and producing salt, forbidding Indians to make their own. Gandhi realized that salt was an essential for Indians, as basic as air and water. Indians, who labored for long hours in the fields, existed on meager fare such as bread and lentils and salt. He saw the government monopoly of this practice as a tax on Indian blood and sweat.

Gandhi (who was called Mahatma Gandhi, meaning "great soul"), was considered the spiritual leader of civil disobedience against the salt laws. His inner voice directed him to lead a Satyagraha, and thus was born the Salt March of 1930. This slender, short man wearing only a loin cloth and holding a staff, marched on foot from Ahmedabad in Bujarat to Dandi, a coastal town 240 miles away, where he announced in advance that he would make salt by extracting it from the sea. He also announced that he would not return home until the government repealed the salt laws.

He walked 10 miles a day, accompanied by disciples and others who joined in, camping at villages and small communities along the way. Someone in the village would bring him a spinning wheel and he would spin wool for an hour, symbolizing his protest against British mill-made cloth. He would then lead a prayer service, calling upon Hindu, Muslim and Christian texts to support the power of nonviolence.

Gandhi and upwards of 70 followers arrived in Dandi on April 5. The next morning they walked into the sea and collected seawater in pans, setting them on the beach where the sun could evaporate the water and make salt. They spent a month making and selling small quantities of salt. As word spread around the world, people throughout India began making their own symbolic marches. One month later Gandhi was arrested in the middle of the night and put into jail, along with other civil disobedience leaders. Not knowing what to do with them, they were released eight months later. Many historians have argued that the Salt March was the beginning of the end of the British Empire. India achieved independence from Britain in 1947.

Gandhi's example inspired many others in countries around the world, who emulated his nonviolent methods of marches, sit-ins and hunger strikes. The American civil rights activist Martin Luther King Jr. marched from Selma to Montgomery in Alabama in 1965; Nelson Mandela spent many years imprisoned in his long fight against apartheid in South Africa; Lech Walesa's Solidarity movement in Poland led a strike at the Gdansk shipyard. The spirit of the law is demonstrated in the bravery of all of these acts. As Martin Luther King Jr. wrote from jail, "An individual who breaks an unjust law that conscience tells him is unjust, and who willingly accepts the penalty of imprisonment in order to arouse the conscience of the community over its injustice, is in reality expressing the highest respect for law. "

Two Heroes Who Helped Save the World

On separate occasions in different parts of the world, two brave and courageous individuals stood up under extremely intense circumstances for what they felt was right – even though it meant going against orders from a commander on the one hand, and against instructions for military procedure on the other. In doing so, these men might actually have prevented the destruction or near-destruction of the Earth and life as we know it.

The first incident involved a Soviet naval officer named Vasili Alexandrovich Arkhipov. In October of 1962, he was in the nuclear-armed Soviet submarine trapped near Cuba by a group of US Navy destroyers led by the USS Randolph. It was the time of the Cuban Missile Crisis. When the destroyers started dropping depth charges, the captain of the submarine, Valentin Grigorievitch, believing that a war might already have started, was ready to launch a nuclear-tipped torpedo.

There were three officers on the submarine who had authority to launch the torpedo if they unanimously agreed on the decision. One of them was Vasili Alexandrovich Arkhipov. Of the three, he was the only one who refused to authorize the attack. He convinced one of the other officers, Savitsky, to bring the submarine to the surface and wait for orders from Moscow. Had a nuclear torpedo been launched, a nuclear retaliation by the US would probably have been inevitable.

In October of 2002 a conference was held in Havana commemorating the 40th anniversary of the Cuban Missile Crisis. Former US Secretary of Defense, Robert McNamara, stated that people were not aware of how close the situation had come to erupting into a nuclear war. The director of the National Security Archives, Thomas Blanton, said that "a guy called Vasili Arkhipov saved the world." It is interesting to note that there was no fan fare. The almost unimaginable catastrophic consequences of a nuclear war were narrowly avoided by the courage of one man who stood firm in his opposition. If a current poll were conducted it is likely that only a small percentage of people would have any idea that we barely escaped a nuclear exchange during the Cuban Missile Crisis.

Another situation with potentially devastating nuclear consequences occurred on September 26, 1983. At that time a Russian Strategic Rocket Forces colonel, Stanislav Yefgrafovich Petrov, was on duty at the Serpukhov-15 bunker near Moscow. Just past midnight indications from his computerized warning system showed that the US had launched a missile that was headed for the USSR. The cold war was still at its peak. Less than a month earlier the Korean Air Flight 007 had been shot down by the Soviets. All 269 people on board were killed. Under the circumstances, Petrov had two choices: he could follow the letter of the law, which would mean immediately notifying his superiors of an impending missile attack against the USSR. Upon such notification an all-out nuclear counter-attack would by launched by the Soviet Union against the United States. It is referred to as the doctrine of Mutual Assured Destruction.

Reasoning that the US wasn't likely to launch just one missile in an attack of this kind, and knowing that the reliability of the satellite system had been questioned in the past, Petrov felt it was more likely to be a computer error. Just a short time later the computer indicated that a second, third, fourth and fifth missile had been launched and were headed for the USSR. Now, with nothing more than his own gut feeling, he still felt that the computer was in error. There was no way for him to confirm the warning, one way or the other. By the time any land radar system could detect an incoming missile it would be too late. If he disregarded the warning and it was in fact true, the Soviet Union would be destroyed by a nuclear attack without any notice or ability to retaliate. The responsibility was totally in his hands. He could fail in his duties. On the other hand, if he reported the computer warning and it was false, a catastrophic attack would be launched against the US. Either way, the lives of hundreds of millions of people were at stake.

Few people have ever been in such a position, where the stakes were so enormous for so many people and the Earth itself. In a few brief minutes he had to make a decision. He took the second choice and decided to trust his intuition. He called the report a computer error. He was right. No missiles attacked that night. With great courage, under tremendous pressure of consequences, he chose to do what he felt was right and ignored protocol.

In the end, Petrov is credited with preventing World War III. This incident was kept secret until 1998. Petrov was not honored or congratulated for his heroic act. After an intense investigation he was considered unreliable as a military officer. He was not punished nor was he rewarded for having prevented perhaps the last great catastrophe on earth. He was reprimanded and reassigned to a lesser post. He later retired from the military to a life of relative poverty.

In 2004 the Association of World Citizens, based in San Francisco, gave Colonel Petrov its World Citizen Award, a trophy, and $1000. In 2006 he was once more honored by the Association of World Citizens in a meeting at the United Nations in New York City. He received small but deserved recognition for enormous courage. All of us alive today, and all generations to come, owe him our gratitude.

If we believe in magic, we'll live a magical life. If we believe our life is defined by narrow limits, we've suddenly made those beliefs real. – Anthony Robbins

Believe that life is worth living, and your belief will help create that fact. – William James

You are what you are by what you believe. - Oprah Winfrey

To believe in the things you see and touch is no belief at all; but to believe in the unseen is a triumph and a blessing. – Abraham Lincoln

Nothing splendid has ever been achieved except by those who dared believe that something inside of them was superior to circumstance. – Bruce Barton

How can you come to know yourself? Never by thinking, always by doing. Try to do your duty, and you'll know right away what you amount to. - Goethe

The greatest use of life is to spend it for something that will outlast it. - William James

I still believe, in spite of everything, that all people are basically good at heart. - Anne Frank

It does me no injury for my neighbor to say there are twenty gods or no god. It neither picks my pocket nor breaks my leg. - Thomas Jefferson

A dream is only as powerful as those who believe in it. - Todd Harrison

All I have seen teaches me to trust the Creator for all I have not seen. - Ralph Waldo Emerson

Be sure you put your feet in the right place, then stand firm. - Abraham Lincoln

To accomplish great things we must not only act, but also dream; not only plan, but also believe. - Anatole France

What the mind can conceive and believe, and the heart desire, you can achieve. - Norman Vincent Peale

CHAPTER 21

Living Good Beliefs

Oprah Winfrey, with all of her wealth and success, says that it is all because she lived her beliefs. "I do believe, I'm a living testimony, that you become what you believe. When people say, 'How did this life, that you see me living on TV and off, happen to me?' I say it's because of what I believed. I really, in the essence of my spirit, know that if I had believed what I was told about myself being colored in 1954 in Mississippi, I could not be here." She didn't take in any of the limiting beliefs or pre-conceived stereotypes that were passed on to her. When she was told that you couldn't be fat and get on television, she didn't believe it. When she was told she couldn't succeed being a woman, she didn't believe it. When she was told she couldn't succeed being a black woman, she didn't believe it. She believed that she would be herself and just let happen what was going to happen. She went with the flow. "That's the number one reason why I've been able to succeed. Because of what I believe."

Whatever your beliefs might be regarding yourself or the nature of God or relationships or anything else, that thing becomes to you what you believe it to be. If you think of God as cruel, punishing, vindictive, and that the universe is based on random chance, you are likely to live in fear, dread and guilt. These negative beliefs attract or create opportunities that seem to demonstrate God's wrath. If you believe that God is compassionate and wise and that the universe is based on balance and harmony, you are likely to live in a state of acceptance and expectancy that will tend to attract blessings and transformation into your life. You will also attract the grace and strength to deal with adversity when it comes. You can replace the word God with relationships or parenting or health and see the same dynamic at work. Every area of your life will tend to reflect your positive or negative beliefs.

The former Czech President, Vaclav Havel, was a poet, playwright and economist. Prior to attaining power he was a dissident and had spent considerable portions of his adult life as a political prisoner. His rise into power came as a result of leading the peaceful Velvet Revolution in 1989. When asked in an interview if he ever felt hatred towards his jailers, he replied: "No, I don't know how to hate, and that pleases me - if for no other reason than because hatred clouds the vision and makes it difficult to seek the truth."

Living good beliefs is fundamental to positive thinking. Good beliefs are those beliefs that empower us, inspire us, and motivate us to learn, grow and express our authentic selves in the world. Whenever we uncover a disempowering belief we have an opportunity to replace it with a belief that better serves our growth and empowerment in the world. For example, if you have a belief that you just "are" a certain way and that's the way it is - you are not smart or you are depressed or you have an explosive temper - then you will live with those disempowering limitations that keep you from meeting your potential and living the fulfilling life you are meant to live.

Beliefs are fascinating and it can be illuminating to explore them. You don't always realize what your beliefs are, where they came from, that they may be conflicting, or that as an adult with a reasoning mind you are able to choose your beliefs and can therefore change them.

One way to begin exploring beliefs is to ask yourself questions: What do I believe about God? Marriage? Relationships? Men? Women? Myself? Death? Afterlife? Even if you think you know the answers to these questions take the time to reflect on them or write them out in your journal, and any other topics that are of importance or interest to you. You may find yourself surprised by what you discover.

The word "remission," for example, was one I (Cheryl) always thought of as something positive – until I was diagnosed with cancer and recovered. Then, when a doctor reviewing my chart asked, "Are you in remission?" I spontaneously said, "Heavens, no! Remission is like having something hanging over my shoulder waiting to pounce back and get me." I realized in that moment that remission is a belief in recurrence, and what we believe in is what we tend to manifest. It was far more empowering to create a positive belief. My new belief is simple: What I know is that today I'm well and in excellent health. I don't know what tomorrow will bring but I will deal with each day as it comes.

Many of the beliefs we hold were taken in when we were young, without mature discerning minds, or from authority figures or influences around us. With maturity we begin to realize that we have the ability to create our own empowering beliefs. Whenever you realize that you're holding yourself back in any area because of a disempowering belief, you can choose to replace it with a positive belief.

When we believe we can do something chances are, if we persist, we will succeed. See yourself achieving what you desire for yourself, take the steps necessary, and celebrate your achievements. There is a formula for success here: Believe, act, and manifest. This formula does not mean that everything you set your mind to, work toward, and manifest, will be easy or even exactly as you imagined. It means that if a goal is realistically possible, it can be done. Chances are it will be done, if you are willing to put forth the effort to make it happen.

Life is not for mere passing pleasure, but for the highest unfoldment that one can attain to, the noblest character that one can grow. - Ralph W. Trine

Character may be manifested in the great moments, but it is made in the small ones. – Phillips Brooks

If I had not been to prison I would not have been able to achieve the most difficult task in life - and that is changing yourself. - Nelson Mandela

Character is the result of two things – mental attitude and they way we spend our time. – Elbert Hubbard

Depend not upon fortune, but on conduct. – Publilius Syrus

Character is the final decision to reject whatever is demeaning to oneself or to others and with confidence and honesty choose what is right. – Arthur Trudeau

If he is to be ultimately at peace with himself, what a man can be, he must be. - Abraham Maslow

With courage you will dare to take risks, have the strength to be compassionate and the wisdom to be humble. Courage is the foundation of integrity. - Keshavan Nair

Integrity is the unwillingness to violate one's own identity. - Erich Fromm

Character cannot be developed in ease and quiet. Only through experience of trial and suffering can the soul be strengthened, ambition inspired, and success achieved. - Helen Keller

Character is like a tree and reputation like its shadow. The shadow is what we think of it; the tree is the real thing. - Abraham Lincoln

In the pursuit of wealth or knowledge or reputation, circumstances have power to mar the wisest of schemes, but where character is the prize, no chance can rob us of success. - Frederich Robertson

You cannot dream yourself into character; you must hammer and forge one for yourself. - James Froude

CHAPTER 22

Building Character and Integrity

The development of character and integrity are necessary steps in the pursuit of finding meaning and purpose. Integrity can be defined as strict personal honesty and independence. According to Stephen Covey, it is the value we place on ourselves and involves being in harmony with our own values. Personal value is that quality of integrity that leads us to live our principles or walk our talk. People with integrity are believable because the inner reality reflects the outer manifestation. It has to do with being able to keep the commitments we make to ourselves, which leads to making and keeping our commitments to others.

Another aspect of integrity has to do with responsibility. We have a core drive to be responsible and contribute in life in a way that benefits the whole, although the circumstances of our environment may blur that drive. In this orderly universe anything that is out of harmony with the principles of balance, compassion and equality is out of integrity. An individual who has grown up in a street-tough environment might exhibit a kind of integrity - a strict personal honesty to "the code" of his familiar existence - but is still out of integrity with some of the larger universal principles. "An eye for an eye" might be an example of adhering to a learned code, while "turning the other cheek" speaks to the higher principle of harmony and compassion.

The building of character and integrity allows us to consider all people with respect. When we fall out of integrity we lose trust between ourselves and others. For example, two people, one of them married to someone else, decide to have an affair. Both are willing to put their desires above their integrity and eventually are found out. The marital partner is crushed, the marriage is dissolved, and the two continue to see each other or even marry. For awhile their mutual complicity might seem to create rapport between them but eventually, each knowing that the other is capable of stepping out of integrity, they will most likely lose trust.

By the actions of our lives, as well as our words, we demonstrate our integrity and generate trust; or we lose it by not treating everyone or every situation by the same set of principles. What may seem to create a bond in the short run, actually communicates a lack of integrity. When we are living in integrity - in harmony with our beliefs and values - we are living the truth as we know it.

Honesty is another component of integrity, but integrity goes a step further. Honesty, of course, means telling the truth. Integrity means telling the truth without deception:

Mom: "Did you brush your teeth?"

Johnny: "Yes."

Johnny's little sister: "You didn't brush your teeth!"

Johnny: "I did so brush them - yesterday!"

Integrity is also acting without deception. A mother brought her young son to Gandhi, a man whose life of integrity is well known. She asked Gandhi to tell the boy not to eat sugar because it wasn't good for him. Gandhi told the woman to bring her son back the following month. When the mother brought the son back Gandhi told him not to eat sugar - that it wasn't good for him.

"Why didn't you tell him when I brought him last time?" she asked.

"Because I first had to stop eating it myself," Gandhi replied.

Withholding the truth is a form of deception as well. If we act behind someone's back in a way that we know would be hurtful to them or our relationship, our relationship is out of integrity. Building integrity means upholding the kinds of principles that build moral strength and character. We may make mistakes but with integrity we can sincerely acknowledge our actions and apologize when appropriate: "I was wrong," or "I was insensitive," or "I made a mistake."

Our character is constantly communicating. As Emerson said, "What you are shouts so loudly in my ears I cannot hear what you say." What we are, our character, communicates much more than what we say or do. Our underlying truth interacts powerfully with those around us, and especially those close to us, even without their conscious awareness.

What exactly is character? In the sense that we are using it, character is that which is aligned with unchanging principles or natural laws. Unlike values, which can be different or shared within certain groups, principles are fundamental and enduring. These unchanging principles include integrity, fairness, harmony, service, and all of the qualities that set a solid foundation for a happy and effective life. When we get our lives into harmony with them, life generally falls into a smoother flow.

One way to further develop character and integrity is to take one step at a time - incorporating into our lives the things that uplift and inspire us, including habits that support our bodies, our minds and our spirits. At the same time we can begin eliminating from our lives the things that bring us down, including habits that don't support our bodies, our minds and our spirits.

Another example that great "characters with integrity" have passed on is that of personal contributions to society. This is something in addition to what is done as a means of livelihood and source of income. And surprisingly, it is often very busy people who find the time to reach out in this way. Viktor Frankl believed that our driving force in life is to find purpose and meaning which transcends our personal lives and brings out the best of human nature. Peace Pilgrim felt that a path of service, something that we do without thought of anything in return, is one of the essential ingredients in creating a fulfilling life. Albert Schweitzer said, "Wherever a man or a woman turns he can find someone who needs him. Even if it is a little thing, do something for which there is no pay but the privilege of just doing it."

Lessons From an Outstanding Coach

Every once in awhile an individual comes along who leaves an indelible impression on those around him. Someone whose attributes exude character and integrity and whose life illustrates our potential to live in harmony with our values. John Wooden, former UCLA coach, was such a person. One of the most revered coaches in the history of sports, Wooden was beloved by his former players, including Kareem Abdul-Jabbar and Bill Walton. Instead of motivating his players through fear or adrenalin producing pre-game pep talks (Wooden believed that adrenalin should be saved for the basketball court), his highest priorities were concern, compassion and consideration. He attempted to spark pride in a job well done and after every game he offered encouraging words, analysis, and advice. Not to say that he wasn't tough on his players. He was strict and demanding. He knew he could be because the team understood that he cared about them. "When players knows you care about them, they will go all out for you."

Wooden had lots of advice for his team members over the years, which he developed into what he called "The Pyramid of Success." He initially chose the cornerstones of industriousness and enthusiasm for the foundation of his pyramid. He chose industriousness because he believed worthwhile things only come from work, and enthusiasm because he felt peoples hearts need to be in what they're doing. In the beginning he didn't know how many qualities or steps it would eventually take to fill in the pyramid. It was finally completed after hundreds of hours of reflection over 14 years. The foundation he laid between the cornerstones were friendship, loyalty, and cooperation. Each was intended to illustrate the importance of establishing a united effort to succeed, defining the power of teamwork.

Building onto the foundation he added self-control, which he considered essential for mastery over emotions; alertness, essential for the acquiring of knowledge; initiative, requiring the courage to make decisions and take action; and intentness, with determination and resolve to stay focused on the objective.

Moving to the third tier he placed condition, skill and team spirit. He deemed these traits to be the heart of the pyramid. Although the words are associated with athletics, he considered them to apply to all individuals. He felt that we must be conditioned – physically, mentally, and morally, to whatever it is we dedicate ourselves to in life; skilled so that we can do our work effectively; and team spirited in giving ourselves to the good of the whole.

Below the peak of the pyramid Wooden placed poise and confidence, which he felt were the result of all of the qualities building up to that point. The goal is to be comfortable with who you are and believe in yourself if you hope to expect others to believe in you.

The crown at the top of the pyramid is success. His intent wasn't to imply winning, but rather knowing that you have given all you have and done the very best you are capable of doing. "What is so important to recognize is that you are totally in control of your success - not your opponent, not the judges, critics, media, or anyone else. It's up to you. That's all you can ask for; the chance to determine your success by yourself," says Wooden, adding, that the Pyramid of Success is more about life than about basketball.

Even though his intent wasn't to equate success with winning, a manifestation of Wooden's principles was that his teams tended to be extremely effective at winning. As head coach of UCLA, he won 10 NCAA national championships in a 12-year period, including seven in a row. No other team has won more than two in a row. During one period his teams made an astonishing record of winning 88 consecutive games. Wooden was named national coach of the year six times.

Wooden credited his own parents for shaping the values he lived and taught. He grew up in a part of southern Indiana where racial intolerance was common, yet his father taught him that all people are equal. He took that lesson to heart and years later when he was told by the National Association of Intercollegiate Athletic Tournament in 1948 that he couldn't bring a black bench player from his university team with him he told tournament officials, "If I can't bring Clarence, we're not coming." His courage to stand by what he knew was right led officials from another college that was the tournament's favorite and biggest draw to also withdraw. Tournament officials then backed down from their racist stand and Wooden 's team, including Clarence, played in the game.

In his 90's, John Wooden continued to learn and enjoyed reflecting on his favorite historical figures, like Abraham Lincoln and Mother Teresa. One of his favorite quotes by the latter is, "A life not lived for others is not a life." He was prolific at coming up with his own "quotable" statements, such as these:

"Discipline yourself and others won't need to."
"If I am through learning, I am through."
"What is right is more important than who is right."
"Don't let making a living prevent you from making a life."
"The time to make friends is before you need them."
"Consideration for others brings many things."

"You have success within. It's up to you to bring it out."

"Never mistake activity for achievement."

"Be quick, but don't be in a hurry."

"Bad times can make you bitter or better."

"Success is never final; failure is never fatal. It's courage that counts."

"Talent is God-given; be humble. Fame is man-given; be grateful. Conceit is self-given; be careful."

An endearing story about John Wooden is told by a friend, about the letters that John wrote on the twenty first of every month after his beloved wife of 53 years died. For more than 20 years he sat down to write her love notes on that special day. He told her how much he missed her, how much he loved her, and that he couldn't wait to see her again. Then he would put the note into an envelope and slip it in the stack of love letters that sat there on her pillow, tied in a ribbon. The letters stayed there, honoring her, while he slept only on his side of the bed. A beautiful tribute to an undying love, offered by a man who embraced life fully and lived his best, continuing to live as an example to others.

Early in John's life a teacher asked, "What is success? How do you achieve it? Who has it?" Throughout his life John Wooden remembered those questions. He pondered them deeply: "These questions really go to what life is all about...The values, ideals, and principals of the Pyramid of Success are the qualities that I believe will allow you to stand tall, now and throughout your days. I've been trying to do that in my own life for over eighty years. I will continue each day to strive for that until the moment the Good Lord calls me to be with my dear Nellie again."

He was called in June of 2010. He was 99 years old. The love, guidance and support he gave to so many will never be forgotten.

The Pyramid of Success

SUCCESS

POISE + CONFIDENCE

CONDITION + SKILL + TEAM-SPIRIT

SELF-CONTROL + ALERTNESS + INITIATIVE + INTENTNESS

INDUSTRIOUSNESS + FRIENDSHIP + LOYALTY + COOPERATION + ENTHUSIASM

Here is a mental treatment guaranteed to cure every ill that flesh is heir to: sit for half an hour every night and mentally forgive everyone against whom you have any ill will or antipathy. - Charles Fillmore

Do not wait for others to forgive, for by forgiving, you become the master of fate, the fashioner of life, the doer of miracles. To forgive is the highest, most beautiful form of love. In return you will receive untold peace and happiness. – Robert Muller

Humbleness, forgiveness, charity and love are the dynamics of freedom. They are the foundation of authentic power. - Gary Zukav

True forgiveness must be extended not only to others, but also to ourselves, and sometimes, in our limited understanding, to the God who we mistakenly believe has singled us out for harsh treatment. - Elinor MacDonald

Not to forgive is to be imprisoned by the past, by old grievances that do not permit life to proceed with new business. – Robin Casarjian

When a deep injury is done us, we can never recover until we forgive. – Alan Paton

Forgiveness is the key to happiness. - A Course In Miracles

Only the brave know how to forgive. A coward never forgives. It is not his nature. – Robert Muller

When Christ says, "Forgive your enemies," it is not for the sake of the enemy, but for one's own sake that he says so. – Oscar Wilde

A forgiving spirit is by its very nature a unifying force. It can remove the barriers of separation between peoples and nations and weld them together in peace and goodwill; something that legislation with the help of armies can never accomplish. – Charles R. Loss

Anger makes you smaller, while forgiveness forces you to grow beyond what you were. - Cherie Carter-Scott

I destroy my enemy when I make him my friend. - Abraham Lincoln

CHAPTER 23

Forgiveness

Blame, guilt and judgment are blocking energies. Forgiveness is a freeing energy that lightens the emotional load we are carrying. It allows us to move forward with the flow of life and creation toward our ultimate good. Forgiveness is a powerful force, not to be underestimated. It is often one of the hardest things to do, but it remains the only real emancipation from many of the chains that hold us back.

"If you want to walk the path of higher consciousness, then you must take a hard look at your own willingness to forgive," Wayne Dyer says. Forgiveness is not easy and for most of us it takes a lot of practice. He also says, "Not to forgive is not to understand how the universe works and how you fit into it." The point is that when you have learned to truly forgive, you have learned to take responsibility for yourself in life. You are who you are, where you are, and how you are, because of the choices you've made, not because of circumstances or how someone outside of you treated you.

Forgiveness allows you to manage your own emotions and not to be manipulated by others. It takes a great deal of self-discipline and if you are willing to put in the effort, results in a growing degree of control over your emotions and thoughts. You don't have to understand or condone hurtful acts by others. You can simply take responsibility for your actions and reactions. That is where your responsibility lies.

Thoughts of blame, guilt, and judgment close the heart and shut us down. Forgiveness opens the heart so that we can flow with that universal or higher energy of love and compassion.

What exists in disharmony outside of us does not have to create disharmony inside of us. The inner world is the one that we do have control over, even if it seems difficult at first.

When you attach cords of resentment to people or situations you are, in essence, tying yourself to those persons and to that pain. Freedom means cutting that cord and trusting God or spirit to bring the person who has hurt or wronged you the experiences he or she needs to heal. Harboring unkind thoughts of vengeance or resentment hurts the bearer of those thoughts more than it hurts the receiver. Why do you have to be the one to forgive when the other person hurt you? Because you are seeking to lift the burden of anger and resentment so that you can be free.

Forgiveness is a healing principle that is espoused by all of the spiritual teachers and leaders, but it can be difficult to fully grasp the concept of forgiveness in a world that gives lip service to these higher principles while endorsing violence and revenge. During one of the many conflicts in the Bosnia/Yugoslavia/Serbia region a group of priests were attempting to get the people to practice forgiveness. "How can you expect people to forgive when they have suffered so much injustice?" a priest was asked by a news reporter. "Because it is the only way out," he responded.

An important aspect of forgiveness is that of forgiving ourselves. We need to learn to forgive ourselves just as we do others. As an example of the ways in which we hold on to guilt and shame, a woman named Mary was in counseling to deal with her fears having to do with an upcoming scheduled surgery. One of her kidneys was full of lesions and needed to be removed. Asked how she felt about the surgery she replied that she felt guilty for not taking care of herself. "Are you doing something that you know is harmful?" she was asked. "Not now," she responded. "But I was an alcoholic and had other substance abuse issues. I've been clean and sober for more than 20 years." She described her sense of shame over the earlier years of self-destructive behavior and her present feelings of vulnerability and lack of control over her body.

During a hypnotherapy session she began to reframe her perspective by first acknowledging and owning the courage and determination she had shown in overcoming years of addiction. Then she was asked to think about and list all of the things that she did have control over in the present situation. As she thought about it she realized that she was in control of the many choices before her. The first specialist she had gone to was newly out of medical school and excited to try a recently developed, less invasive procedure with doctors in training at a teaching hospital. Mary felt she was being pressured and had a negative gut reaction. She went to another specialist who was well experienced in a more invasive procedure that had proven to be very successful. Even though she wasn't thrilled about the more invasive surgery, she felt good about this doctor and confident in his experience. She made a decision to go with the second doctor.

Mary had made another very important choice right after her diagnosis. Regardless of the outcome of surgery (whether or not the removed lesions were cancerous), she made a firm decision to retire from her very stressful job. She had a sense that there was something else, something important, that she needed to do with her life. As she talked she realized that the immediate reaction she'd felt when she heard about the condition of her kidney was that she was going to be all right. And she was pleasantly surprised to find that she had even more loving support from her family, friends and colleagues than she had anticipated.

When Mary looked at the vulnerability and fear she was feeling, she realized it was coming from the inner child part of herself. She also had a strong, confident and courageous adult part. After a hypnotic visualization she opened her eyes and said, "It's not my fault. I've been under a lot of stress at work for several years and I was just trying to do a good job." As she continued to acknowledge her self-forgiveness, and to nurture and integrate all the parts of herself, she was no longer afraid. When the surgery came around she was prepared for it. The energy that had been holding her in fear and self-judgment was released and freed, enabling her to heal more rapidly. It is in the act of following the higher principles we believe in – like forgiveness – that we find the peace and healing we seek, both in our lives and in the world.

Let us rise up and be thankful, for if we didn't learn a lot today, at least we learned a little, and if we didn't learn a little, at least we didn't get sick, and if we got sick, at least we didn't die; so, let us all be thankful. - Buddha

If you can't have what you want, be grateful for what you have. Keep thinking constantly of all the big things you have to be thankful for instead of complaining about the little things that annoy you. - Dale Carnegie

When we are grateful for the good we already have, we attract more good into our life... When we are ungrateful, we tend to shut ourselves off from the good we might otherwise experience. – Margaret Stortz

Gratitude is one of the great positive emotions because it creates magnetism. A magnet is that which draws things to itself; therefore, by giving heartfelt thanks for all the good we now have, through the magnetism that gratitude creates, we will start attracting more good into our daily life. – Elaine Hibbard

You can praise a weak body into strength; a fearful heart into peace and trust; shattered nerves into poise and power; a failing business into prosperity and success; want and insufficiency into supply and support. – Charles Fillmore

To create something new, or to keep receiving more of something you have already gotten, get some paper and pens and write a thank you to the Universe. – Sanaya Roman

A grateful thought toward heaven is itself a prayer. – Rudolph Bock

Gratitude is a vaccine, an antitoxin, and an antiseptic. – John H. Jowett

I thank God for my handicaps, for through them, I have found myself, my work and my God. – Helen Keller

Gratitude unlocks the fullness of life. It turns what we have into enough, and more. It turns denial into acceptance, chaos to order, confusion to clarity. It turns a meal into a feast, a house into home, a stranger into a friend. - Melody Beattie

CHAPTER 24

The Practice of Gratitude

The practice of gratitude awakens the heart and contributes to a life of abundance. The kind of abundance we're talking about, true abundance, is a richness in the way we view and receive life, not an accumulation of things. Gratitude and abundance are interconnected and often lead to simplicity. Simplicity removes the clutter so that we can view with joy the beauty and the blessings that surround us.

A way to become aware of the abundance we already possess is to begin a practice of gratitude. To quote Philippians 4:8, "Finally brethren, whatever is true, whatever is honorable, whatever is right, whatever is pure, whatever is lovely, whatever is of good repute, if there is any excellence and if anything worthy of praise, let your mind dwell on these things." Few activities bring such immediate reward as developing a routine practice of reviewing all of the abundance that is surrounding us in our lives at this very moment.

Let's say, for example, that you experience a "bad" day. The kids brought home less than perfect grades on their report cards, the car broke down on your way to work and by the time you got there you missed that important call you had been hoping would come in. Here it is the end of the day and even your body, with drooping shoulders, is reflecting your mood. There is nothing like gratitude for a quick pick-me-up.

Find a quiet room or draw a warm bath and settle in with your gratitude journal. Start with the obvious. Your health, the health of your spouse and children. Yes, the kids are noisy and boisterous.

You can just see them bouncing up and down with all that vitality. Thank God.

Your life is busy, you rarely see your spouse alone except for when you go to bed at night and then you're so tired you both fall right to sleep. But you can just feel that comforting togetherness when you imagine his/her warm hand that always finds your shoulder in the middle of the night. Thank God.

The grass isn't mowed and it surely needs it but you can remember when you never dreamed you would ever own your own home much less the great yard that came with this one. Thank God.

The car broke down but you were able to pick it up on your way home from work and now it's fixed. It'll probably give you months of trouble-free transportation before more maintenance is needed. And you did miss that call but the fact that it came in is a good sign. You can keep working on it. Life is good. You never know what each new day is going to bring.

Does it really matter that the kids' report cards weren't perfect? Of course you want them to grow and develop into all they can be. You want them to be happy. How wonderful that they have all their faculties intact. They have the ability to learn and enjoy life. If they need a little extra help or incentive in school, fine. Having perfect grades isn't the goal. Helping them to be all that they can (not what you want them to be) is what counts.

The kids are expecting a harsh lecture but what else might you do? What are you proud of them for, for example, before you remind them of how much you know they are capable of, maybe even more than they realize? You feel yourself smiling at their probable surprise to your new approach. And your partner. How will he/she react when you look at him/her with these eyes of gratitude?

Our friends, Eric and Ellen, play a gratitude game that they call "If only... but WAIT!" One of them will pick a bad outcome that didn't actually happen, and then they get to "magically" reverse it to what really did happen. For example, Ellen might say to Eric, "If only I'd stopped at the grocery store last night for eggs, then I wouldn't have to go out in the cold this morning... but, WAIT! I did get eggs last night and I don't have to go out!" Then they dance around happily enjoying their fun. This game was devised from the wisdom of Thich Nhat Hanh, a Vietnamese Buddhist monk, who points out that when you have a toothache, all you can think about is how happy you would be not to have the toothache; now, you can enjoy that same happiness without having to have the toothache first.

For a variation, how about seeing the good we already have with fresh eyes: "If only I could wake up this morning and have a wonderful, magical life full of beauty, joy, and wonderful relationships. But WAIT! I do!"

When we forget to be grateful we tend to shut ourselves off from the good we might otherwise experience, but when we're grateful for the good we already have it tends to multiply. Make up your own Gratitude Bulletin Board and update it regularly:

I am thankful for...

...the flowers in spring because they lift my spirit and remind me that life is a celebration.

...good friends because it is so satisfying to have trusted companions to share in the joys and sorrows of life.

...my livelihood because it gives me the means to provide my family and myself with the comfort of a good home and a healthy environment.

...a sense of humor because it's fun and allows me not to take myself or things too seriously.

...my children because they bring out the nurturing and strong parts of myself that have shown me how capable I am of loving and giving.

...my partner because he/she has taught me to receive love as well as give it - and through whose eyes I can more easily see my own value and worth.

...the wriggling body and wagging tail of my dog because he is so welcoming when I come home, no matter how tired or cranky I might be.

...the sound and feel of Velvet's vibrating purr because it is so relaxing when I sit down exhausted at the end of the day.

...my mind with all of its capabilities and complexities because it is unfathomable in its potential.

...the health and strength (and yes, beauty) of my body because it allows me to move, dance, and fully experience and participate in the physical world.

An extra bonus to practicing gratitude is that it has been shown to:

- Stimulate the immune system
- Lower blood pressure (even more so with a grateful cat on your lap)
- Improve sleep
- Increase closeness in relationships
- Encourage altruism

Prayer indeed is good, but while calling on the gods a man should himself lend a hand. - Hippocrates

Pray as if it all depends on God, but work as if it all depends upon you. – George W. Carver

Prayer is not a vain attempt to change God's will: it is a filial desire to learn God's will and to share it. Prayer is not a substitute for work: it is the secret spring and indispensable ally of all true work. – George Buttrick

Communicating with God is a deep inner knowing that God is within you and around you. God "speaks" through the still small voice within. – Peace Pilgrim

Let us not pray to be sheltered from dangers but to be fearless in facing them. Let us not beg for the stilling of the pain but for the heart to conquer it. – Rabindranath Tagore

Steady, determined and purposeful action is one prayer always answered. – Norman Thornton

A single grateful thought towards heaven is the most complete prayer - Minna von Barnbelm

In prayer it is better to have a heart without words than words without a heart. – John Bunyan

Prayer is like the turning on of an electric switch. It does not create the current; it simply provides a channel through which the electric current may flow. – Max Handel

Prayer is not flight; prayer is power. Prayer does not deliver a man from some terrible situation; prayer enables a man to face and to master a situation. – William Barkley

To see our work as prayer and an opportunity to bring forth a flash of truth is a great gift. To know that even the busy world is a holy world is quite a change of heart. - Dhyani Ywahoo

It is for us to pray not for tasks equal to our powers, but for powers equal to our tasks, to go forward with a great desire forever beating at the door of our hearts as we travel toward our distant goal. - Helen Keller

CHAPTER 25

Making Prayer Powerful

Prayer can be described as a spiritual communion with God or spirit. There are many forms and traditions surrounding the concept of prayer. It can mean a devout repetition of traditional prayers within a particular religion, a petition for a certain outcome in a given situation, a declaration of worship or devotion, an expression of gratitude, or a deep receptive silence, among others. A great deal of satisfaction is often experienced by those who pray regularly, regardless of the form it takes.

An exploration of prayer can help to expand the practice of praying into an even more potent and positive force. Prayer originates as a thought, and a consciously directed thought can be very powerful.

In the beginning we might think of prayer as a petition for something we want. With our limited perspective, however, not getting what we want might be a blessing. As Teresa of Avila cautioned, "More tears are shed over answered prayers than unanswered ones." Or as the saying goes, "Be careful what you pray for. You might get it."

A Gallup poll taken in the United States revealed that 95% of people reported a belief in God and 76% reported that they pray on a regular basis. If three quarters of us are using prayer, then most of us have some belief in a divine source. Faith or belief in a higher power usually comes with a sense that God or spirit is an omniscient Being - who knows our needs without having to be asked. How then can we make prayer more powerful?

Imagine that prayer is a direct line to God. If you could actually have God on the other end of this direct line do you really want to tell God what you want? Or do you want to ask for direction and guidance in following your authentic path? Prayer becomes powerful when we begin to open our inner ears and make a clear connection with that highest source of guidance in our lives.

Another way that we sometimes pray is to ask for the removal of some physical or emotional problem, or some situation or circumstance that we or a loved one may be facing. It's difficult, but we can learn to step back into a more objective perspective. We don't generally see the bigger picture. Prayer can help us open up to an awakening of our higher natures - as opposed to the lower or self-centered nature. From this broader perspective we can begin to trust that the difficulties and problems that come in life come for a reason, even though we don't usually see that reason in the moment. It is in retrospect that we can often look back and see all that we have learned and how far we've come as a result of facing the challenges that come our way.

When you accept that whatever comes is for your own growth and learning, or to give you an opportunity to be of service, then your prayers may refocus from asking for the removal of a symptom or situation, to asking for courage and direction. When you face your problems squarely you have an opportunity to learn and grow through the solving of them, rather than postponing the lesson or opportunity that has come to you or a loved one.

Praying for others has been shown to be very powerful and those prayers which are open-ended, focused on the removal of cause and not the removal of symptoms or disease, may be even more effective. A powerful prayer of visualization for a loved one or someone in need, is to send love in the form of light or compassion. You might imagine that the individual being prayed for is becoming open and receptive, perhaps imagining the person's face and arms uplifted and receiving. In your mind's eye you can also lift that person into God's hands. Then you can leave the individual there, knowing he or she is in the best possible hands. The following story is an example of such a prayer:

Susan's family had been split for many years due to a falling out that had happened between her and her sister, Ann. Although Susan felt in her heart that she had not done anything wrong, the recent near death of their mother, who had suffered a heart attack, brought home to her that life is transient and the time of departure unknown. Years earlier Ann had become very upset by Susan's choice to move to a new location that offered her a better position than the job she had, which was in a company that Ann also worked for. Ann had called her selfish, among other things, and said she was no longer a member of her family – and was not welcome to associate or be in contact with her or her children. Ann had never recanted and years went by. Presents sent by Susan in the beginning were returned unopened.

Years passed and then Susan decided to use a prayer of visualization each day, seeing Ann and her family surrounded by light and sending her loving good wishes. After a few months of this Susan felt inspired early one morning to write to her sister and share her thoughts about how short and fleeting life could be, and how heart-broken she would feel if something were to happen to one of them and they had never talked or seen each other again. Susan didn't mention the reason for their years of separation but instead reminisced about shared childhood memories, and ended by telling Ann that she would always be grateful to her for stepping in to take care of her when she had been ill and debilitated for almost two months. She sent the letter off with hope for a reconciliation, but no expectations. She left the outcome in higher hands.

Only days later Susan received a phone call from Ann. No mention was made of their years of separation. Ann talked of having a family gathering on the upcoming holiday. The members all came together, and no mention was made of the time that had lapsed. No blame and no formal apologies were ever exchanged. Susan accepted that Ann wasn't, and might never be, ready to talk about what had happened. She was able to let it go and the reconciliation "took." The family was able to reestablish their cohesive unit and bonds.

Knowing how to pray when we see a loved one suffering can be very difficult, and never more so than when a mother feels helpless in the face of a child's suffering. Kalie Morino told a story about her son who was dying of a terminal illness. The day after she received word from his doctors that his condition was terminal, Kalie had a heart attack. Her heart stopped beating and she had a near death experience in which she saw an angel. It was a beautiful and peaceful state in which she found herself, but when she was given a choice, she made the decision to come back.

The experience was a turning point in her life, a gift really, as such experiences can be, because she no longer feared death. She knew that if her son died he would be fine. She even knew that it would be a beautiful experience of being in the loving arms of God, as she had just experienced.

She now was able to recognize that she didn't know what was best for her son. She turned to God and asked, "What should I do? I only want what is best for my child, no matter what that is. What should I be praying for?" The thought that came to her was, "Just love him. If he is to die, your love will help him to make the transition, and if he is to live, your love will heal him."

This answer was so simple. Kalie knew that she could be with her son and just love him. She went back to the hospital that day just loving her child with all of her heart and soul, knowing that her love would make a difference no matter what the outcome. As she entered the hospital room he was playing with soldiers in his crib, in spite of a high fever. His soldier had just been shot and he picked it up and was holding it very lovingly in his arms. "That's right," Kalie said, "love him, honey. Love heals."

The little boy looked up surprised and said, "It doesn't matter, mommy. He'll just be born again." Kalie looked at him in shock, having had no idea that he understood such a concept. Because of his answer and obvious acceptance of death, she assumed that he was probably going to die, so she spoke to him about letting his soldier follow the light. "What light?" he asked. Kalie pointed up and said, "The light of God." He stared up into the air transfixed, saying, "Mommy, it's bootiful!" He was so transfixed she thought he was leaving right then.

A nurse entered shortly after to take him to a lengthy bone marrow test but returned with him in less than an hour to announce that his blood platelets had miraculously returned to normal. The doctor told Kalie her son had gone into remission but not to get her hopes up, as he would most likely be back and die within the month. Instead, Kalie's son, David, grew up to have two children of his own. Love is a powerful healing prayer.

Beauty, as it is reflected in nature or music or art is also something that, as we begin to grow an awareness of, can open that connection to God or spirit. Walking in receptive silence in the beauty of nature, in that sense, is a prayer. Wonderful inspirations can come and to make prayer powerful, inspirations must then be put into action. The same is true of inspiring music or art. Inspiration is an emotion that takes us to a higher level - an expression of our authentic selves. By authentic selves we mean that part of us that is in harmony with universal principles. Whenever we are expressing that higher aspect of ourselves, we are putting our inspiration into action. Certain music or art may have the ability to open the energy of the heart, for example, which might lead to a softening or compassion concerning someone for something we've been harboring resentment toward, or a more accepting attitude toward some situation which has been challenging.

Gratitude, discussed in the previous chapter, is another form of prayer. Used regularly, it can make profound changes in our inner lives. Gratitude as a prayer is a form of positive thinking and your thoughts have everything to do with what you manifest in your life.

The prayer of gratitude can be practiced in many ways. Gratitude can be expressed in written form in a daily journal, in the inner reflection of morning or evening meditations, or in the development of an attitude that you bring into your awareness regularly during the day. To some, the visual experience of a daily journal may bring the sense of gratitude to a deeper level, while for others the act of closing the eyes and bringing the experience into an interior stillness deepens the prayer. It's good practice to try both ways and get a feel for which might be most effective for you. Both experiences open the channel that begins to bring that sense of prayerful gratitude into more moments of the day.

"Praying without ceasing" has been described by various mystics as being in a state of constant gratitude and outgoing positive thought. Whenever we express beauty or compassion or love we are opening ourselves in prayer and accessing a connection to our highest potential.

All action begins at the center - in silence, the sacred space where true discovery resides. – Maitreya

Settle yourself in solitude, and you will come upon God in yourself. – Teresa of Avila

The more powerful and original a mind, the more it will incline towards the religion of solitude. – Aldous Huxley

Only when one is connected to one's own core is one connected to others. And, for me, the core, the inner spring, can best be refound through solitude. – Anne Morrow Lindbergh

Nowhere can you retire with more quietness or more freedom than within your own spirit. Constantly give yourself to this retreat, and renew yourself. – Marcus Aurelius

Prayer begins by talking to God, but it ends by listening to Him. In the face of Absolute Truth, silence is the soul's language. – Fulton J. Sheen

We spend a great deal of time telling God what we think should be done, and not enough time waiting in the stillness for God to tell us what to do. – Peace Pilgrim

Before embarking on important undertakings, sit quietly, calm your senses and thoughts, and meditate deeply. You will then be guided by the great creative power of Spirit. – Paramahansa Yogananda

True meditation gives us, as it were, wings for flight to a higher realm and thus detaches us from terrestrial fetters. – Paramananda

No great work has ever been produced except after a lone interval of still and musing meditation. – Walter Bagehot

Silence gives us a new way of looking at something. – Mother Teresa

The purpose of meditation practice is not enlightenment; it is to pay attention even at extraordinary times, to be of the present, nothing-but-in-the-present, to bear this mindfulness of now into each event of ordinary life. – Peter Matthiessen

What a strange power there is in silence. – Ralph W. Emerson

CHAPTER 26

Time Alone in Receptive Silence

Life can be busy and overwhelming with demands. We're bombarded by outside distractions, noise and activity, mind-numbing television or video games, deadlines and commitments. Yet there is one sure-fire place we can go to get calm, clear and connected. It is in the silence - alone, undistracted and undisturbed. Quiet time alone is not a luxury. For the spiritual seeker, it is a necessity.

What is the spiritual life? It is life lived from an awareness that we are much more than a physical body. In fact, we are not our physical body at all. The body is a suit of clothes or vehicle that houses that part of us that never dies - the spirit. That is the spark that activates the body during our time in this life.

When we keep ourselves busy on the external side of life, never allowing ourselves to go into that quiet, perhaps even afraid of what we might find if the noise stops, we may attempt to fill the growing void with all kinds of distractions. The void is the silence, calling us. It is the still, small voice within that is being drowned out. It nags us to be still and listen. We may have become apprehensive about trusting that inner realm of sensing. In a materialistically oriented society, the inner life is not always given value or validation.

Receptive silence connects one to a state of mystical perception. The mystic is one who, through the practice of receptive silence, experiences a direct connection with God or spirit. The mystic pursuit is that of transforming one's self into an integration of body, mind and spirit, guided by spirit. The rewards of this journey allow us to develop a growing sense of serenity and freedom from anxiety and frustration. As we become more attuned to ourselves, we become more attuned to others.

Delving into this inner realm expands our understanding of the deep meaning and spiritual dimension of life. A catastrophic situation or condition has the potential to propel one toward this inner quest, as can a profound mystical or religious experience. Over time the mind becomes clearer, confidence grows, and even health may be improved. That is not to say that the spiritual path is an easy one. When a spiritual path is embarked upon, the road is very challenging. It brings great opportunities to further one's strength, conviction and faith.

Spiritual perception begins within, and then manifests outwardly. Perceptions may have to do with clarifying beliefs and attitudes that have been negative or that have held you back in any way. Or that have made you feel separate or limited. It is a time of self-discovery. You learn that what you have perceived as problems are actually lessons in self-awareness. This becomes the goal: to know yourself.

As Maitreya put it, "Everyone needs 'inner space' where there is no one directing you, telling you where to go and what to do. You have been given that space so that the confusion and chaos around you will dissolve. You must never surrender that space to anyone, except your true self. Meditation is really a journey back to that space to find peace and happiness."

In order to make use of this great tool of receptive silence or meditation, a daily practice is recommended, in which time for quiet is set aside. Not only do you get the benefit of becoming calm and more mentally alert and clear, but this time devoted to inner practice recharges your energy and boosts your immune system. Some responses are immediate and apparent, while others develop gradually. Immediate improvements might be a reduction in stress and tension. This can be enhanced by a process of slow, deep breathing and conscious relaxation as you let go and enter the quiet. It can be done within the context of self-hypnosis. Overall feelings of peacefulness, energy and mental clarity are common. Betty Bethards said, "With daily meditations we can pack in twenty years' worth of lessons in one year's time."

Although meditation is often thought of as a time of sitting quietly, even in specific postures, there are many ways to meditate and many ways to enter receptive silence. When you enter a true state of meditation, body awareness fades into the background until you lose awareness of it. Emotions become serenely still. The mind enters a peaceful state of stillness – waiting, but not pushing. This is the receptive silence that connects you with deep inner receiving. For those who aren't comfortable with sitting meditations, the same state can be reached in walking meditations, preferably alone in a beautiful natural setting. Peace Pilgrim used to say, "From the beauty of nature you get your inspiration, from the silent receptiveness you get your meditation and from the walking you get not only exercise but breathing – all in one lovely experience." She also said it's important to put whatever insights come to you into practice. The purpose of receptive silence is to become open to higher receiving so that you can find your unique direction and purpose in life.

Robert Adams described silence as the ultimate reality: "True silence really means going deep within yourself to that place where nothing is happening, where you transcend time and space. You go into a brand new dimension of nothingness. That's where all the power is. That's your real home."

The return from your work must be the satisfaction which that work brings you and the world's need of that work. With this, life is heaven, or as near heaven as you can get. Without this - with work which you despise, which bores you, and which the world does not need - this life is hell. - William Edward Burghardt

When our inner self connects to our work and our work to our inner self, the work knows no limit, for the inner self knows no limit. – Matthew Fox

One of the most durable satisfactions in life is to lose one's self in one's work. – Harry E. Fosdick

It doesn't matter what you do – as long as you do it with love. – Mother Teresa

The path of love and the path of insight lead into the same garden. – Stephen Mitchell

I've come to believe that each of us has a personal calling that's as unique as a fingerprint - and that the best way to succeed is to discover what you love and then find a way to offer it to others in the form of service, working hard, and also allowing the energy of the universe to lead you. - Oprah Winfrey

Don't aim for success if you want it; just do what you love and believe in, and it will come naturally. - David Frost

Success is not the key to happiness. Happiness is the key to success. If you love what you are doing, you will be successful. - Herman Cain

When love and skill work together, expect a masterpiece. - John Ruskin

The most important motive for work in school and in life is pleasure in work, pleasure in its result, and the knowledge of the value of the result to the community. - Albert Einstein

The definition of professional nirvana is to do what you love with people you respect while serving the greater good. - Todd Harrison

Work is love made visible. – Victor Frankl

CHAPTER 27

Doing What You Love

Each of us brings into this world our own creative talents and interests and it is those very inclinations that point the direction to our path of fulfillment. We discover meaning and purpose in life by pursuing the creative endeavors that we love, that express our values, and that contribute in a positive way to society and the world.

Each one of us has a special calling or role to play. When you don't know what your calling is you can turn to your inner guidance – the voice of your personal truth and wisdom within. We are always being guided. All we have to do is open ourselves to this direction and follow it with diligence and perseverance. Practices such as meditation or journaling or self-hypnosis can be a link to that inner voice.

A calling is a summons that comes from the highest part of yourself and is based on something that you enjoy doing; something that is beneficial to society. It doesn't have to be a big thing, in fact most of us are called to small things. Mother Teresa said, "It may not be possible for an individual to do great things in this world; all one can do is small things with great love."

When something is a calling the motivation behind it is positive and beneficial. You enjoy doing it, even if it entails hardships. Being a teacher or a realtor or a janitor can be a calling, as can being a musician or forest ranger or parent. It isn't what you do so much as what motivates you that is important. If your motivation is primarily for money that wouldn't constitute a calling. You may make a lot of money but you won't feel satisfied in a deep and meaningful way. If your motivation is primarily to be of service you may still make substantial amounts of money, but you will feel great satisfaction knowing that others are benefitted as well as yourself.

Changing jobs is one way to find a more fulfilling livelihood, although it isn't always necessary. If what you're doing is something that is useful to society but you don't feel fulfilled, you might experiment with a change in motivation or attitude toward the work you do. Ask yourself what it is you are working for. If your answer is money, a change in motive might drastically alter your sense of enjoyment. A positive motive would include a sense of purpose in what you are doing. Peace Pilgrim tells the story of a truck driver who met her after hearing her talk on the radio about having endless energy. "I had that once," he said. "It was when I was stranded in a town because of a flood. I got inspired to help out and I worked without eating and without sleeping and I just had that endless energy. But I don't have it anymore." "Well what are you working for now?" she asked. "Money," he replied. "That should be quite incidental," she told him. "You have that endless energy only when you are working for the good of the whole." Satisfaction and enthusiasm come when you begin working with the motive of providing a needed and valued service.

If the work you are doing isn't personally satisfying or useful to society you may need to change jobs. If you aren't aware yet of what it is you are called to do, you can turn to your inner guidance to begin to find direction. Hypnotherapy or self-hypnosis can be a beneficial way to gain insight. The purpose of hypnosis in this case is to still the conscious mind through relaxation and tap in to the deep resources of the subconscious mind and higher awareness. The subconscious, the seat of all of your memories and emotions, is a great place to gather information about what it is in life that really sparks your enthusiasm and passion. What are the things that you really enjoy? These are clues. Connecting to that inner awareness can inspire you in the direction of your personal calling and place in life.

As you get information you can begin to put it together to find the path that will lead to meaning and purpose in life – both professional and personal. Silence or walking meditation is another beneficial practice to open up to inner guidance. When looking for inner direction you can walk in some quiet, beautiful place. It can be helpful to bring a pad and pen to jot down any inspirations or ideas that come so they aren't forgotten.

Journaling is yet another way to enter the subconscious mind and higher awareness. Get a note pad and pen and pose a question, such as What is my right job or occupation? Or What do I really love to do? Just start writing down whatever thoughts come. You can also take the inspirations or ideas that come out of a session in hypnosis or meditation and begin journaling to develop them. Whenever you receive inspiration it is important to act on it. If you don't move your inspirations into action, they become unrealized potential.

Questions lead to answers. You can ask questions when you meditate and then become quiet and receptive; you can ask questions when you go to bed at night and then drift into sleep knowing that the subconscious part of your mind remains alert to direction from your higher awareness. Answers come from all kinds of sources: a sudden moment of insight, a relevant dream, a person who says something that strikes an inner confirmation, and so on.

Whatever process or processes you might use, the important thing is that you begin to put into action the ideas and inspirations that come. Just take little steps and as you move forward more doors will begin to open. If you find yourself drawn to something but you're not qualified, you might enroll in a course or read a book to see if it really holds your interest and sparks your passion. Experiment, search, and have fun.

The following story from Peace Pilgrim: Her Life and Work in Her Own Words, illustrates how we find clues from the things we enjoy doing that help us to put together a meaningful life that includes finding our right work:

I'll give you an example of a woman who had some difficulty finding out what her job was in the divine plan. She was in her early forties, single, and needed to earn a living. She hated her work to the extent that it made her sick, and the first thing she did was to go to a psychiatrist who said he would adjust her to her job. So after some adjustment she went back to work. But she still hated her job. She got sick again and then came to me. Well, I asked what her calling was, and she said, "I'm not called to do anything."

That was not true. What she really meant was she didn't know her calling. So I asked her what she liked to do because if it is your calling you will do it easily and joyously, as I walk my pilgrimage. I found she liked to do three things. She liked to play the piano, but wasn't good enough to earn her living at that. She liked to swim, but wasn't good enough to be a swimming instructor, and she liked to work with flowers.

I got her a job in a florist shop so she could earn her living working with flowers. She loved it. She said she would do it for nothing. But we used the other things too. Remember, she needed more than just a livelihood. The swimming became her exercise. It fits in with sensible living habits. The piano playing became her path of service. She went to a retirement home and played old songs for the people there. She got them to sing, and she was good at that. Out of those three things such a beautiful life was built. She became a very attractive woman and married a year or so later. She stayed right in that life pattern.

I don't know what your destiny will be, but one thing I do know: the only ones among you who will be really happy are those who have sought and found how to serve. - Albert Schweitzer

Not everyone can be famous, but everyone can be great. For greatness is determined by service. - Martin Luther King, Jr.

One of the things I keep learning is that the secret of being happy is doing things for other people. – Dick Gregory

Great opportunities to help others seldom come, but small ones surround us daily. – Sally Koch

The service of man(kind) is more valuable than what you call "service to God." God has no need of your service. Please man, you please God. – Sathya Sai Baba

The worst days of darkness through which I have passed have been greatly alleviated by throwing myself with all my energy into some work relating to others. – James A. Garfield

The great happiness in life is not to donate but to serve. – Louis Brandeis

We make a living by what we get, we make a life by what we give. - Winston Churchill

Joy can be real only if people look upon their life as a service, and have a definite object in life outside themselves and their personal happiness. – Leo Tolstoy

There is nothing you cannot do, no defeat you cannot survive, no fear you cannot overcome, when you are concentrated heart and soul in helping others. – Robert O'Brian

When we serve and when we give, we open ourselves to receive life's richest blessings, its greatest prizes, and its most enduring successes. – Henry T. Hamblin

All other pleasures and possessions pale into nothingness before service which is rendered in a spirit of joy. – Mohandas Gandhi

The way you begin to change the world is through service. – Martin L. King, Jr.

CHAPTER 28

The Value of Service

Nature teaches many lessons pertaining to physical law. She is also a great teacher of spiritual lessons, which we see when we look a bit deeper. The laws which operate in the physical world also operate in our minds and lives. What we sow on a mental level we reap in our lives – just as in nature the tiny acorn grows into the majestic oak.

If you were to ask a farmer planting barley what crop he expects to harvest he will laugh at the absurdity of such a question. He knows that if he plants corn he will grow corn, that an apple seed will grow into an apple tree, and that like springs forth from like.

Such certainty is also the unseen reality of service. It is a spiritual law that what you give out is returned to you – in a rich harvest. It is impossible to give without receiving in return, even the most prized possessions such as health, happiness and inner peace. When service is the motivation behind action it creates a magnetic attraction. It is an outgoing energy that leads to spiritual treasures.

A side-effect of serving or contributing in some meaningful way is the raising of self-esteem and satisfaction in life. What each person contributes makes a difference in the world. Knowing that you can make a difference gives a sense of purpose and meaning to life.

The idea of doing something to be of service can seem overwhelming, especially when caught in the rush of time-pressured lives. But true service doesn't have to be about time. It can be about maintaining a positive attitude and motivation that is giving and outgoing. It is one of the aspects of a fulfilling life that leads toward a sense of balance and purpose. It is an attitude that you can carry with you anywhere. A good reminder of how influential attitude can be is the saying, "What goes around comes around." From a self-centered focus: The boss chews you out, you go home and scream at the kids, the kids go out and are mean to their friends. When ill will is projected it spreads. The same principle is at work on the positive side. When calmness or compassion is projected, it spreads. What you give out is attracted into your life.

You are always creating your experience of the world. Service acts like a magnet, attracting an abundance of good will and balance. You can take it into the work place, call on it when driving a car, or practice while standing in a busy grocery store line. Since it is an outgoing energy your focus changes from a self-centered perspective to an outgoing perspective – how you can offer support to those around you. Imagine the difference in developing an outgoing perspective in any of these areas:

At work, instead of thinking about just getting your work done or what you'd rather be doing or what you're going to be doing after work, you focus on giving the task at hand your best attention and effort; you maintain awareness of those around you whether co-workers, clients or customers, and offer positive communication.

When driving, you stay vigilant and offer an attitude of cooperation. If someone is trying to move over into your lane you can slow down and let them in. If someone is going too slow you can pass safely when appropriate and remain polite. Treat every driver on the road with respect, even when they seem distracted or rude.

When waiting in a busy line, be aware of the stress levels of those around you. Imagine what the clerk must deal with each day and be a source of good will and cheer. Easiest of all in any situation, a smile offered to a stranger does wonders to lift the spirit. The giver of outgoing positive energy is as refreshed as the receiver.

Acting on an attitude of service can also help to dispel feelings like the lethargy of depression, the despair of grief, or spirit deadening self-pity. Whenever you find yourself caught up in the kind of energy that is draining you can pull yourself up by doing something for someone else or for something you believe in. Getting involved in any meaningful act that is for the benefit of others (including yourself) boosts the spirit with rewards that vastly outweigh the effort.

The flip side of being of service is allowing yourself to be a gracious receiver when you find yourself in circumstances in which you may need to rely on the generous help of others. That was particularly brought home to me (Cheryl) when I had cancer and was living in public housing. I was surrounded by elderly and variously challenged individuals who appeared at my door for a kind word or appreciation, and in turn they showered me with gifts in the form of food or flowers or small treasures. And if word got around that I wasn't up and about on a particular day neighbors would come by, hobbling on artificial hips or leaning on canes, to offer to bring me whatever I might need from the store. As I watched worn faces light up when I mentioned needing something at the store and saw the satisfaction with which an extended item was brought to me, I realized that my most valuable service to them might have been allowing them to be of service to me.

The examples given illustrate that contributing in a positive way isn't something that needs to be done on a grand scale. Service is most of all an attitude that can be developed by looking around and seeing what needs doing in your home, your community, your country, and the world. We are all capable of contributing to the collective well being. Developing an attitude of service can and does effect both our internal world and the world around us.

Go confidently in the direction of your dreams. Live the life you have imagined. – Henry David Thoreau

Whatever we expect with confidence becomes our own self-fulfilling prophecy. - Brian Tracy

It is difficult to make a man miserable while he feels he is worthy of himself and claims kindred to the great God who made him. – Abraham Lincoln

Confidence stems from positive beliefs about yourself; it does not depend upon the approval of another person. – Author unknown

Skill and confidence are an unconquered army. – George Herbert

Make the impossible possible, the possible easy, and the easy elegant. – Moshe Feldenkrais

No one can make you feel inferior without your consent. - Eleanor Roosevelt

One can never consent to creep when one feels an impulse to soar. - Helen Keller

If you develop the absolute sense of certainty that powerful beliefs provide, then you can get yourself to accomplish virtually anything, including those things that other people are certain are impossible. - Anthony Robbins

Confidence, like art, never comes from having all the answers; it comes from being open to all the questions.- Jack Gibb

You can't connect the dots looking forward; you can only connect them looking backwards. So you have to trust that the dots will somehow connect in your future. You have to trust in something - your gut, destiny, life, karma, whatever. This approach has never let me down, and it has made all the difference in my life. - Steve Jobs

I feel this great creative and spiritual force within me that is greater than faith, greater than ambition, greater than confidence, greater than determination, greater than vision. It is all these combined. My brain becomes magnetized with this dominating force which I hold in my hand. - Bruce Lee

CHAPTER 29

Confidence and Vision

We limit ourselves by thinking that things can't be done. The difference between succeeding and failing is often pretty slim. When the going gets really tough we can either give up or push on one more time - and the "one more time" just might be the one that pushes us past the obstacles. Thomas Edison, who patented more than a thousand devices, including the phonograph and the incandescent light bulb said, "Genius is one percent inspiration and 99 percent perspiration."

We are what we think ourselves to be. The good news is that if the image we have of ourselves is not the way we want to be, we can change by changing our image. We can put our awareness outside of ourselves and observe objectively, and we can go inside ourselves and feel the truth of our emotions. We can change. The choice is ours. We can react - that is, give in to the conditioning of our habitual patterns and let circumstances push us and pull us in whatever direction the wind is blowing; or we can call on that part of ourselves that separates us from other species - and make a conscious choice about the kind of person we choose to be.

Confidence and vision come from having the courage to remain conscious, and to make a fully intended decision to become what we choose to be. It takes risk, meaning a chance of loss, not only of internal or external security but the letting go of thoughts that hold us back from following our passions. There is always an easy way. For example, it may be easiest to do nothing. The easy way isn't bad or good, it's just not a path that leads us to our inherent potential to do and be all that we are capable of doing and being. The path that taps us into that potential may seem risky. Confidence comes from doing it anyway. When we first started pulling ourselves up onto furniture it was risky, but we did it. We must have fallen many times yet in the end we learned to walk. If we had given up the first time we tried and fell (or the eighth or ninth) we wouldn't be walking today. We have all had an experience, many experiences, of building confidence and success.

Steve Jobs is an excellent model of confidence and vision. His achievements can be seen as a beacon of light, paving the way for expanding our confidence in following the beat of our own inner drum. Jobs dropped out of college and was fired from his position as a tech executive, and went on to transform the world's experience of personal computers and phones. He taught us that making mistakes can sometimes lead to the best possible outcome as we follow our visions with confidence.

If you are not doing today what you want to be doing because you think you lack confidence, it may be only the thought that is holding you back. Confidence doesn't come without first facing your fear about something or of the unknown. You face whatever it is that is unfamiliar or that frightens you, and then do it anyway. How many excellent public speakers started out with confidence? There are some who are outgoing and seemingly fearless by nature. But many started out with some trepidation and went on to speak in front of an audience anyway.

As a young man in England, Gandhi was elected to the Executive Committee of the Vegetarian Society and attended all of the meetings – but he was tongue-tied. He once wanted to address an important topic that was coming up so he wrote notes that he could read. When the time came he couldn't bring himself to even read what he had written and had it read by someone else. In any social setting, the presence of half a dozen people or more would strike him speechless.

After studying law he found that he was good at gathering facts but was hesitant at his ability to present them. When he got up the courage to take a case (because he needed the money) he made his debut in small claims court, where he had to cross-examine witnesses. His mind went blank and he couldn't think of any questions to ask. He resigned on the spot. Yet he came to find his confidence and he certainly found his vision. He later said,

"Beyond occasionally exposing me to laughter, my constitutional shyness has been no disadvantage whatsoever. In fact I can see that, on the contrary, it has been all to my advantage. Its greatest benefit has been that it has taught me the economy of word. It has allowed me to grow. It has helped me in my discernment of truth." Gandhi, admittedly shy, had no confidence in his ability to communicate his thoughts, yet he forged ahead and changed a nation. Even after death, his life work continues to inspire millions.

When you face your fears you realize that your catastrophic expectations don't come to pass. "I thought I would die!" But it didn't happen. And when you make it through some difficult situation you start to trust that you can do it again – and again. It may not be easy, but then it may be easier than you think. Your reactions to the experiences of life are determined by your thinking, which you can change. "Yes, I'm scared. But I can do this."

You have the creative ability to build confidence and vision into every area of life. Everything exists in the mind first and then comes into being through action. What motivates you and fills you with enthusiasm? What do you love? You can look at this question in regard to what you do for your living, the kind of relationships you would like to have, where you would like to live, what kind of environment you would like to live in, what inspires you, what you do that inspires or serves others, and so on. Every day you can do something - take one step - in one or more areas of your life to move closer to your visions, growing in confidence as you do so.

What we focus on we tend to manifest, and as we resolve to move toward the things we love the universe begins to move with us - and may even add magical dimensions to our vision of what can be. As Saint Francis said, "Start by doing what's necessary; then do what's possible; and suddenly you are doing the impossible."

Don't let others discourage the potential of your vision:

1859: "Drill for oil? You mean drill into the ground to try and find oil? You're crazy." -Drillers that Edwin L. Drake tried to enlist in his project to drill for oil.

1872: "Louis Pasteur's theory of germs is ridiculous fiction." - Pierre Pachet, Professor of Physiology at Toulouse.

1876: "This 'telephone' has too many shortcomings to be seriously considered as a means of communication. The device is inherently of no value to us." - Western Union internal memo.

1895: "Heavier-than-air flying machines are impossible." - Lord Kelvin, president, Royal Society.

1899: "Everything that can be invented has been invented." - Charles H. Duell, Commissioner, US. Office of Patents.

1929: "Stocks have reached what looks like a permanently high plateau." - Irving Fisher, Professor of Economics, Yale University.

1943: "I think there is a world market for maybe five computers. " - Thomas Watson, chairman of IBM.

1962: "We don't like their sound, and guitar music is on the way out." - Decca Recording Co. rejecting the Beatles.

1977: "There is no reason anyone would want a computer in their home." - Ken Olson, president, chairman and founder of Digital Equipment Corp.

1981: "Cellular phones will absolutely not replace local wire systems." - Marty Cooper, inventor.

1995: "I predict the Internet will soon go spectacularly supernova and in 1996 catastrophically collapse." — Robert Metcalfe, founder of 3Com and co-inventor of Ethernet.

1997: "Apple is already dead." – Nathan Myhrvold, Microsoft CTO.

2005: "There's just not that many videos I want to watch." - Steve Chen, CTO and co-founder of YouTube expressing concerns about his company's long term viability.

2007: "There's no chance that the iPhone is going to get any significant market share." -Steve Ballmer, Microsoft CEO.

The purpose of life is a life of purpose. - Robert Byrne

We are all designed for a purpose; we all have something for which each of us, and each of us alone, is responsible. – Naomi Stephan

The great need of our times is for people to be connected to spirit; for people to be connected to a core of feeling in themselves that makes their lives vital and full of meaning, that makes life a mystery evermore to be uncovered. – Harold Stone Sandplay

To have a purpose that is worthwhile, and that is steadily being accomplished, that is one of the secrets of a life that is worth living. – Herbert Casson

Divine purpose for us is learning to live in harmony with God's will. – Peace Pilgrim

Learn to get in touch with silence within yourself and know that everything in this life has a purpose. – Elisabeth Kubler-Ross

Those who have failed to work toward the truth have missed the purpose of living. – Gautama Buddha

Strong lives are motivated by dynamic purposes. – Kenneth Hildebrand

People say that what we're all seeking is a meaning for life... I think that what we're really seeking is an experience of being alive, so that our life experiences on the purely physical plane will have resonance within our innermost being and reality, so that we can actually feel the rapture of being alive. - Joseph Campbell

Although a man may have no jurisdiction over the fact of his existence, he can hold supreme command over the meaning of existence for him. - Norman Cousins

The great and glorious masterpiece of humanity is to know how to live with a purpose. - Montaigne

I learned at least this by my experiments. That if one advances confidently in the direction of his dreams and endeavors to live the life which he has imagined, he will meet with a success unexpected in common hours. - Henry David Thoreau

CHAPTER 30

Finding Meaning and Purpose

Existentialism, a philosophy of existence that stresses responsibility for one's own actions, says that to live is to suffer, and to survive is to find meaning in the suffering. While we can't tell someone else what his or her purpose is, we each have to find our own purpose and accept responsibility for the path we uncover. Nietzsche said, "He who has a why to live can bear almost any how."

Viktor Frankl, a psychiatrist who survived life in a concentration camp and wrote the classic *Man's Search for Meaning*, discovered that when all else is stripped away what alone remains is, "the last of human freedoms – the ability to choose one's attitude in a given set of circumstances." In his later practice he attempted to awaken individuals to a sense of being responsible to life for something, however challenging their circumstances in life might be.

Among the dozens of books that Frankl authored, he originally intended to publish Man's Search for Meaning anonymously in order to convey to the reader "that life holds a potential of meaning under any circumstances, even the most miserable." When teaching his students he would caution them, "Don't aim at success – the more you aim at it and make it a target, the more you are going to miss it. For success, like happiness, cannot be pursued; it must ensue, and it only does so as the unintended side-effect of one's personal dedication to a cause greater than oneself...." Frankl was pointing out that when one follows a calling to "a cause greater than oneself" it leads to a sense of purpose or the finding of meaning in life.

Peace Pilgrim was referring to the same principle when she spoke about the importance of motive in whatever it is that we are doing. "If your motive is to find inner peace for yourself you will not find it. The motive, if you are to find inner peace, must be an outgoing motive. Service. Giving, not getting. Your motive must be good if your work is to have good effect. The secret of life is being of service."

As you seek meaning and purpose your awareness begins to expand and you come to recognize that there is an invisible force that has always been there in the background. That force may have given you direction, challenged you, or gotten you through some crisis. In retrospect you may realize that there were times when you bypassed opportunities or acted against an inner knowing. You may have been tired or afraid or too attached to a person or material things to move on when you knew from inside that it was time. While you could languish in regret or guilt, hanging on to such feelings is painful and unrewarding.

The gift that comes with maturing discernment is that it is never too late. When you recognize that you have lost your path you can choose to reenter it. The distractions of the outer life cause many to disconnect from the deep reality of their inner connectedness and wholeness. Finding your connection to the source or the sacred is not something that can be approached through the intellect. It isn't visible and it cannot be scientifically measured. It is something that is felt and understood from within. It brings comfort and peace.

Painful or catastrophic situations sometimes serve to break down personal barriers and open one to question the deeper verities and realities of life. A book by Charles Yale Harrison called *Thank God for My Heart Attack* addresses how a life-threatening event can pose a challenge: how to redesign your life so that it fits you, rather than you attempting to fit into it. Supreme joy and happiness can do the same. However you come to it, when you are ready certain questions seem to bubble up from the deep stillness within and can be the catalyst that redirects you to that core of inner wisdom. They are spiritual questions having to do with why you are here on Earth and what unique gifts you might have to develop and share. When you begin to seek answers to these questions you embark on a sacred path – the finding of your sense of purpose and direction.

As you begin or extend your journey you may be led to different spiritual tools that help you to wake up the intuitive part of the mind and stir within your heart the longing for connectedness and remembrance of your purpose in life. Certain tools may seem to call to you personally. They might include meditation, self-hypnosis, inspiring music or books, walking in the beauty of nature, or yoga. You may find books or teachers that speak in ways that touch an inner sense of confirmation or rightness. You can study the things that come to you, find the universal principles contained within, and make them your own.

The spiritual path teaches you to know and trust that there is a higher guidance available to you, helping you to learn and grow. As Peace Pilgrim put it, "Pray directly to the source, then be open to guidance however it comes." It comes in many forms: a recognition of synchronicities in occurring events or meetings, such as the uncanny appearance of a teacher or book or idea at just the right time; a heightened awareness that allows one word or the glimpse of a dream image to lead to an insight or "Aha!" experience; an emergence of patterns or symbols that impart a sense of the sacred or convey a personal sense of direction. This compassionate guidance might urge you to risk comfort and reach for meaning in your life. If you reach deep enough you may even find that the resources you need suddenly appear, obstacles dissolve, and you find yourself "in the flow."

As you walk your path you also learn to find the touchstones that put you in contact with your inner knowing. For some it might be an inspiring natural setting, or sharing with friends or like-minded groups, or beautiful music or art. When you walk a spiritual path you find the importance of returning to the touchstone that inspires you, lifts you up, and directs your focus within. You awaken to a longing to know yourself, to discover and own your gifts, and to take action in the world.

Our primary relationship is really with ourselves. Our relationships with other people constantly reflect exactly where we are in the process. – Shakti Gawain

The false promise is that another person giving you love will solve your problems, make you happy, give you the security you desire, make you feel good about yourself. – Jordan & Margaret Paul

When we enter into any relationship with the premise that we are empty and the other person will fill us in, we are sure to fail. We can only win when we proceed from wholeness. – Alan Cohen

Love does not consist in gazing at each other, but in looking outward in the same direction. – Antoine de Saint-Exupery

Powerful relationships arise when two centered individuals commit themselves to unconditionally love one another and to support each other's growth toward full potential. – Thomas Crum

Two persons thinking of each other's happiness will find themselves sharing a rich store of durable satisfactions. – Leland F. Wood

I have learned not to worry about love; but to honor its coming with all my heart. - Alice Walker

The most empowering relationships are those in which each partner lifts the other to a higher possession of their own being. – Teilhard de Chardin

Relationships are part of a vast plan for our enlightenment. – Marianne Williamson

A relationship is like a garden. If it is to thrive it must be watered regularly. Special care must be given, taking into account the seasons as well as any unpredictable weather. New seeds must be sown and weeds must be pulled. – John Gray

In life you'll realize there is a purpose for everyone you meet. Some will test you, some will use you, and some will teach you. But most importantly, some will bring out the best in you. - Author Unknown

Each friend represents a world in us, a world not born until they arrive, and it is only by this meeting that a new world is born. - Anais Nin

CHAPTER 31

The Lesson of Relationships

Good relationships begin with the relationship you create with yourself. You have to get it right with yourself in order to get it right with others. Are you the person that you want to be? Is the image that you project on the outside true to your inner self? This is the lesson of relationships. They reflect back to you those areas in which you have developed strength as well as those areas in which you have an opportunity to learn and grow. When you tap into your inner core of consciousness and begin to relate from your authentic self, you find that the world, including your closest relationships, begin to relate to you more positively and deeply.

You can use all kinds of relationships - work, friendship, intimate, to gather information about your relationship with yourself. The interactions in your outer life can be like a mirror, giving you access to the state of your inner being. Do you inspire respect in your relationships? If you tend to be an underdog, you may need to learn to give respect to yourself before you can start attracting it from others. If you tend to be a top dog, perhaps you need to practice extending respect to others. Whatever qualities you would like to have in a relationship, you need to develop first in yourself.

Relationships serve many purposes in our lives. Some come into our lives for a short time, others for a longer period or a lifetime. They might offer us support or guidance when we need it, help us through a particular difficulty, or assist us physically, emotionally, or spiritually. These are the relationships that are easy to appreciate.

Others may come into our lives and seem to offend us, or just when we feel secure they abandon us. A partner might choose to leave or he or she might die. Other relationships might challenge us until we find the courage to move past judgment or to take a stand. Even when relationships come with difficult dynamics, we can usually step back in time and realize that they taught us valuable lessons. All relationships serve some purpose. They teach us, broaden our perspective, give us an opportunity to grow, or give us an opportunity to be of service.

Sometimes, when we have an important lesson to learn, we fall into a pattern in relationships that keeps repeating itself. Most of us can pick out an acquaintance or friend, if not ourselves, who has gone through a series of relationships that keep coming to the same impasse or issue. It might be a personal relationship or work-related, but some pattern persists and will continue to come up for that individual until that particular lesson is learned. Dr. Phil, author of Relationship Rescue, encourages people "to scrape away life's layers of distortion and get back in touch with their own core of consciousness, so they can stop sabotaging their relationships and let go of the pain, guilt, anger and confusion."

Before you work on a relationship outside of yourself you may first need to get clear with yourself. If you feel there is a void inside that needs someone from outside to fill you up, you may enter into a relationship feeling needy - you want something from the other person that the other cannot fulfill. Ultimately, you will find yourself disappointed. The lesson is to work on what you need to do to feel whole within yourself, ready to be interdependent with another whole person.

Whether special relationships come into your life for a period of time or a lifetime, you can learn to tarry in those places and enjoy what you have to teach and learn from each other. If the time comes to move on you can let go and move on lovingly. Other people may come into our lives for a lifetime and share life-long lessons. They are often the building blocks of our emotional foundation. You can learn to love the people that come into your experience and accept and use the lessons of all of your relationships to develop your highest potential, thereby aligning yourself with your authentic self.

Stephen Covey, author of The 7 Habits of Highly Effective People, related the following conversation with a participant at one of his seminars:

"Stephen, I like what you're saying. But every situation is different. Look at my marriage. I'm really worried. My wife and I just don't have the same feelings for each other that we used to have. I guess I just don't love her anymore and she doesn't love me. What can I do?"

"The feeling isn't there anymore?"

"That's right. And we have three children we're really concerned about. What do you suggest?"

"Love her."

"I told you, the feeling just isn't there anymore."

"Love her."

"You don't understand. The feeling of love just isn't there."

"Then love her. If the feeling isn't there, that's a good reason to love her."

"But how do you love when you don't love?"

"My friend, love is a verb. Love - the feeling - is a fruit of love, the verb. So love her. Serve her. Sacrifice. Listen to her. Empathize. Appreciate. Affirm her. Are you willing to do that? Proactive people make love a verb. Love is something you do: the sacrifices you make... Love is a value that is actualized through loving actions."

If you are in a troubled relationship you may feel some resistance to bringing the work back to yourself. "Why me?! I'm only half of this picture and I'm the one who always has to do the work!" But you are, and always will be, the only person that you can change. Change yourself and the relationship will change, either moving closer or moving away. That is both the risk and the opportunity.

As roles within personal relationships continue to shift on the collective level, it has become even more challenging to figure out the rules and learn the lessons that relationships have to teach us. In this emerging contemporary age, as individuals strive to define their roles within a relationship, we may find ourselves defining new paradigms. Ideally, relationships are partnerships in which both parties share the responsibility of creating a working model. Without awareness and effort, boundaries or responsibilities within the relationship may become blurred. There are no longer any hard and fast rules. We're left on our own to figure things out, to discover where it is that our strengths and weaknesses lie, and what we can contribute to the relationship and to our partner. (The relationship can be viewed as a separate entity that is created out of the choice to come together with another individual.)

For a life-long intimate partnership to be mutually empowering certain elements are necessary, like respect, commitment, trust, acceptance, and love. It takes genuine willingness to develop sensitivity to your partner even when (and especially because) you see things through the filter of your own history, experiences and belief systems. If you are happy within a relationship but your partner is not, perhaps the relationship has been set up to meet your needs and not your partner's. If you are the unhappy partner then perhaps your needs are not being met - and you have a responsibility to communicate your needs in an appropriate way. Part of the process of creating a supportive and loving relationship is finding realistic solutions through compromise and negotiation that nurture the spirit of both partners.

Mutual respect is the cornerstone of all healthy relationships, whether with partners, children, friends or co-workers. A lack of respect damages not only our core energy and spirit, but that of our relationship. When we treat ourselves or others with disrespect we become cold and hard, often critical and nit-picking. Those who receive our disrespect, especially those close to us like partners or children, become handicapped in their ability to express positive feelings, to achieve their potential, to feel worthy, to feel success even when it is achieved, or even to build healthy relationships. When you respect yourself and others your core energy and relationships are nurtured and can grow in healthy, positive ways. Those around you are likely to become more able to express positive feelings in return, to adapt more easily to the stresses in life, and to accept success.

Commitment is an agreement to share the joys and sorrows that come along, to offer your strength when your partner feels weak or vulnerable, and to know that you can draw on the strength of your partner when you feel vulnerable. It is an agreement to put aside your ego, your preferences and your personal comfort when need be, in respect of and deference to the nurturing of your partner's and your own maturity and growth. It is an agreement to set aside conditions, "I will love you if..." and know that you are serving your own growth by serving the growth of your partner. The deepest and most soul satisfying relationships are formed when the growth and emotional well-being of both partners takes precedence over the desires of either individual.

Acceptance may seem obvious, but all too often people enter into relationships with the idea that they can change the other person. This attitude leads to great disappointment as the reality that the only person you can ever change is yourself, sets in. In truth, the very things that you try to change in a partner are most likely going to become the things that your partner rigidly holds on to.

The time to decide whether or not someone will make a suitable partner is before a commitment is made. If someone has different values or behaviors or attitudes that are unacceptable or deal breakers in a long term partnership, face that reality before making promises that may compromise your integrity or ability to keep. If you choose to enter a committed relationship accept that your partner is okay just as he or she is. You will not only find your own peace, but you may find your partner more malleable to compromise as you let go of the need to control. Letting go of the impulse to change each other leads to a deepening sense of acceptance and trust.

Trust allows us to remain open to giving and receiving the love that we have for each other. High levels of trust enable us to communicate in ways that allow for mutual empowerment and resolutions that provide a winning solution to both partners. Low levels of trust thrust us into a dynamic of defensiveness in which the goal is to win or be right at the expense of our partner losing or being wrong.

Relationships based on higher principles and maturity dissolve the need to build up ego defenses and open the way for trust. The goal is always that of serving the highest good of each partner and the relationship. Since we can't possibly serve each other through deceit or subterfuge, we can be free to trust. And the flowering of these characteristics - unconditional acceptance, commitment, and trust - allow us to more fully develop those inner attributes of character and integrity that are the stepping stones of good relationships in all the areas of our lives.

The kind of love that we are capable of generating in a relationship is something that develops as a result of loving actions. We may not always agree but we remain willing to negotiate and to listen to each other. Sometimes we may need to weigh the passion of our partner's needs against our own and make compromises - but always we stay with our choice to love. We can be angry or sad or of a different opinion, but our goal is to love - not to be right or to gain advantage.

Love, perhaps the most powerful force in the universe, grows over time when given the right conditions. Love the feeling becomes something warm, familiar, trusted, enduring, and secondary to love, the verb. For example, you might come home tired and looking forward to your own quiet space, but finding your mate in distress you put aside your tiredness to listen sympathetically or get dinner ready for the kids. The Hollywood version of love is depicted as a feeling that we have little control over but love is always a choice. When the stepping stones of respect, commitment, trust and acceptance have been laid out in action, the love within us expands and endures - even through challenging and difficult times.

Remember the three R's: Respect for self; Respect for others; and responsibility for all your actions. - Anthony Robbins

I think that feelings waste themselves in words; they ought to be distilled into actions, and into actions which bring results. – Florence Nightingale

There should be less talk; a preaching point is not a meeting point. What do you do then? Take a broom and clean someone's house. That says enough. – Mother Teresa

Our deeds determine us, as much as we determine our deeds. – George Eliot

All the beautiful sentiments in the world weigh less than a single lovely action. – James Russell Lowell

The real compensation of a right action is inherent in having performed it. – Seneca

Blessed are they who translate every good thing they know into action, for ever higher truths shall be revealed to them. - Peace Pilgrim

Do what you can, with what you have, where you are. – Theodore Roosevelt

Knowing is not enough; we must apply! Waiting is not enough; we must do. – Goethe

You may never know what results come from your actions, but if you do nothing, there will be no results. Everything you do may seem insignificant, but it is of the greatest importance that you do it. - Gandhi

They get farthest in the realm of character-building who link up thought and action, who do not merely dream but act upon their noblest imaginings. – R. W. Wilde

Think like a man of action, act like a man of thought. – Henri Bergson

A little knowledge which you carry into action is more profitable than much knowledge which you neglect to carry out into action. – Hermes

CHAPTER 32

Response-Ability

Response-ability is the capacity we have as human beings to respond to our surroundings with integrity, even when our actions are not seen or known. Because we have been endowed with free will we don't always choose to respond with integrity, thus we experience imbalance and challenging lessons on both personal and collective levels. If we could see with a broader perspective we would embrace the truism that what goes around comes around, otherwise known as the law of cause and effect. Ultimately, we will realize the consequences of our actions.

An Indigenous people's understanding of responsibility and consequence was clearly penned in The Constitution of the Iroquois Nations, a five nation alliance or confederacy that some say was written as early as 1390. In any case, it was well before any European invasion or association. Early arrivers found that the Iroquois had been well established in a self-governing society for many generations. They acknowledged a Creator or Great Spirit and had a strong sense of family which was organized and led by the women. Their constitution stated: "In our every deliberation we must consider the impact of our decisions on the next seven generations." The wisdom of "The Great Binding Law" that was written into that Constitution is something we could well learn from in modern times, where corrupt and short sighted policies have promoted the dwindling and dying of our natural resources and the integrity of our collective health and well-being.

As a people, we have grown away from an awareness of our connection to the earth and the consequences of that lack of awareness have become far-reaching. Collectively, we have disregarded the impact of our actions on mother earth and future generations. We have further distanced ourselves from the reality of our consequences by providing many choices that avoid responsibility for our dwindling resources and energy sources and have the potential to destroy us.

One of the most lethal and long term legacies currently being generated is the accumulation and stockpiling of nuclear waste. As the world searches for alternatives to fossil fuels such as coal and oil, agents that contribute to global warming, the nuclear industry is raising its toxic head. Nuclear plants like Sellafield in Britain and la Hague in northern France each process 5,000 tons of spent nuclear fuel each year, which is approximately one third of annual global output. China is planning to add 30 new nuclear plants by 2020, India has plans to build several more, and Iran has been hoping to break into the playing field. The sludge that is left after plutonium and uranium have been removed from spent fuel rods emits 40 times a lethal dose of radiation. The sludge is then cooked down into a powder, mixed with molten glass and poured into stainless steel urns. These urns are then sealed in insulated steel containers and stored. Finally, these containers are buried in areas that are considered to be geologically stable.

The half-life of plutonium is 24,000 years. That means it will take 250,000 years to degrade completely, leaving growing areas uninhabitable. There is no end to the generations that will be affected by the toxic waste that is building up today. How did we let this happen? What accountability is there for those responsible for the (mis)leading of civilization in this manner? Some scientists say they are confident they have the answers on waste. That assumption is based on a short-sighted perspective that is willing to gamble with the quality and sustainability of life on this most beautiful and ailing planet.

We need to protect our ability to live healthfully on a healthy planet not only to the seventh generation, but to the unending potential of life. It is up to all of us not to allow the catastrophic potential destruction voiced by U Thant to become prophetic: "As we watch the sun go down, evening after evening, through the smog across the poisoned waters of our native earth, we must ask ourselves seriously whether we really wish some future universal historian on another planet to say about us: 'With all their genius and with all their skill, they ran out of foresight and air and food and water and ideas,' or, 'They went on playing politics until their world collapsed around them.'"

To those who see with loving eyes, life is beautiful. To those who speak with tender voices, life is peaceful. To those who help with gentle hands, life is full. And to those who care with compassionate hearts, life is good beyond all measure. – Author Unknown

The life that goes out in love to all is the life that is full, and rich, and continually expanding in beauty and in power. – Ralph W. Trine

Give away your love, freely and without expectation. Give it away, and soon your life will be filled with love, and you will have set others on the path of love and peace. - John Robbins

Though we travel the world to find the beautiful we must carry it within us or we find it not. – Ralph w. Emerson

Thoughts of lack manifest as limitation. Thoughts of abundance manifest as success and happiness. Failure and success are but two ends of the same stick. – Ernest Holmes

The course of human history is determined, not by what happens in the skies, but by what takes place in the hearts of men. – Arthur Keith

The crises of our time, as we are beginning slowly and painfully to perceive, is a crisis not of the hands but of the hearts. – Archibnald MacLeish

A fine heart is a fountain of gladness, making everything its vicinity to freshen into smiles. – Washington Irving

You find all within yourself that you find without. The world that surrounds you is the magic glass of the world within you. – John K. Lavater

There is no difficulty that enough love will not conquer. There is no disease that enough love will not heal. No door that enough love will not open. No gulf that enough love will not bridge. No wall that enough love will not throw down. And no sin that enough love will not redeem. It makes no difference how deeply seated may be the trouble. How hopeless the outlook. How muddled the tangle. How great the mistake. A sufficient realization of love will dissolve it all. And if you could love enough, you would be the happiest and most powerful person in the world. - Emmett Fox

CHAPTER 33

How the Inner Reflects the Outer

We are subject to psychological laws in the same way that we are subject to physical laws. Physical law, like that of gravity, is easier to see and accept. When we throw a ball into the air it will come down. Psychological laws are not always easy to see, but are reflected in the concept that like attracts like. If our inner condition is depressed, for example, we may not see or accept the correlation that our own state of mind is the cause of "seeing things gray." When we cultivate a positive mental attitude, we find that doors begin to open - perhaps in ways we didn't dare dream of.

The influence of the mind can be so subtle as to be unnoticed, yet with awareness that same influence can be phenomenal. I had a friend once who had a knack for finding four-leaf clovers. "I don't get it," I told her. "How do you do it?" She said it was easy. "You just have to become aware of four-leaf clovers." Still, it seemed too difficult and there wasn't that much clover growing around me. So I decided to become aware of heart-shaped rocks. It was amazing. Once I became "aware" of heart shaped rocks they were everywhere. My collection grew until I didn't know what to do with all of them. Then everywhere I went I kept finding heart-shaped objects. I think there is great humor in the universe. Heart shapes started manifesting regularly in the clumps I was removing from my cat's litter box! Eventually I forced myself to stop looking for heart-shaped rocks while I was out walking because my eyes would compulsively look down and revel in these discoveries to the degree that I was missing much of the scenery.

The moral might be that we often don't see what we're not looking for. Thought is the beginning of creation. What are the things that you want to see in your life? Thus you can use the power of positive visualization to attract positive things. That is the utilization of psychological law. The inner condition - our thoughts and feelings - reflect or manifest in the outer. We have much more potential than we realize.

That being so, to what degree can you control your thoughts? Perhaps more than you realize. Depression, anxiety and fear are not feelings that most people would identify as wanting to keep or have more of. Yet we get stuck in them and often vehemently deny that there is any way out. There is truth in the saying that the way out is through, and there are many ways and many tools to get through something. The more you learn about what works for you, the sooner you can begin to change your inner experience and in so doing, reflect that change into your outer experience.

Meditation is a tool that many have discovered to have a transformational effect on consciousness. Meditation is a stilling of the mind. There are many methods to attain a state of inner quiet and a number of benefits from doing so. Benefits attributed to meditation include more clarity of mind, a lessening of anxiety, greater serenity, vitality and creativity, all of which begin to reflect into our outer experience.

A state of mindfulness or meditation can be achieved while walking, working, or engaged in some sport or activity, but it might be best learned and cultivated initially by stilling the body in a state of relaxation. Sitting is usually preferable to lying down so that the body can be relaxed without the mind falling asleep. Uncrossing the arms and legs allows circulation and energy to flow more freely. One way to begin is to do a progressive relaxation, beginning at the head and moving down to the feet. Or the reverse, beginning at the feet and relaxing each group of muscles as you work your way up. After relaxing the body you can focus on your breath. In the beginning you might do that for 10 or 15 minutes. When thoughts intrude just allow them to float through and out, bringing your focus back to your breath. A mantra or meaningful phrase can also be used to keep the mind focused and still. An example would be to think the words, "My mind is becoming clear and quiet," with each inhalation and, "My body is relaxed and at ease," with every exhalation.

Self-hypnosis is similar to meditation in that it takes the mind into an altered or focused state but adds the benefit of directed visualization and positive suggestion. It is another tool that can be cultivated to give you more access to the untapped resources of your mind. Self-hypnosis can include the progressive relaxation mentioned for meditation along with further techniques, such as counting down from 20 to one, and giving yourself suggestions to relax deeper with every number. "Number 20, relaxing deeper and deeper, number 19, deeper with every number that I count," and so on until you reach the number one, "Completely relaxed." Once deeply relaxed you can ask your subconscious mind to bring memories to the surface of times when you were feeling the feelings you want to resurrect: calmness, confidence, happiness, a peak experience.

From this place, reconnected to positive feelings, you can direct your imagination, also a function of the subconscious mind, to visualize the good things that you would like to see happen in your life. You can also visualize how you would like to respond in the event that you need to confront certain challenges. An interesting fact about the subconscious mind is that the images in a visualization can evoke the same emotions, sensations and experience as an actual event, which is what makes positive suggestions in a state of self-hypnosis so powerful. It is an extraordinary tool that uses psychological law to change disempowering beliefs and replace them with empowering ones.

Another example of how the inner state of our consciousness reflects the outer is prayer. Prayer is a way of communicating our thoughts, hopes, needs or dreams to a higher power or God. Although an earlier chapter addresses ways to make prayer powerful, there is no correct way to pray. Truth lives within us and prayer is a connection to that inner truth. It is also a great relief sometimes, after we have done all we can in a certain situation, to lift the situation and any overwhelming feelings to God or higher hands, in prayer. Again, prayer is powerful psychological law. It can align us with an inner sense of order and peace that can then begin to manifest on the outside as well.

If you want to develop your awareness of how the inner reflects the outer, consciously follow your feelings through a day when you leave the house angry or upset, versus a day when you leave feeling on top of the world. Keep a notebook or journal handy to note your experiences and interactions throughout the day. On which day are you likely to be aware of the beauty around you or your love of your work or your family, friends or nature? To create more days filled with an awareness of the good fortune and love in your life, keep a gratitude journal or notebook. Write in it every day to remind yourself of the beauty around you that reflects your awareness of the beauty within. Just a sentence or two, written daily, can begin to influence and enhance your experience of life.

Don't waste yourself in rejection, nor bark against the bad, but chant the beauty of the good. - Ralph Waldo Emerson

The music that can deepest reach, and cure all ill, is cordial speech. – Emerson

Cheerfulness is the best promoter of health and is as friendly to the mind as to the body. - Joseph Addison

There is no physician like a cheerful thought for dissipating the ills of the body. - James Allen

Eventually you will come to understand that love heals everything, and love is all there is. - Gary Zukav

Love is the great miracle cure. Loving ourselves works miracles in our lives. - Louise Hay

Love cures people — both the ones who give it and the ones who receive it. - Dr. Karl Menninger

True forgiveness is one of the most healing, releasing and freeing gifts we give to ourselves. - Brandon Bays

Drag your thought away from your troubles... by the ears, by the heels or any other way you can manage it. It's the healthiest thing a body can do. - Mark Twain

If you want to enjoy health, start this very moment to cleanse your consciousness of all wrong thinking and rid it of every thought except the thought of LOVE. - James B. Schafer

To become a thoroughly good man is the first prescription for keeping a sound mind in a sound body. - Francis Bacon

A strong body and a bright, happy or serene countenance can only result from the fine admittance of thoughts of joy and goodwill and serenity into the mind. - James Allen

The closer man associates himself with nature, the greater his personal, spiritual and even physical well being grow and expand as a direct result of that association. - Frank Lloyd Wright

CHAPTER 34

Sewing the Seeds of Good Health

Stress is experienced when we are under mental, emotional or physical strain and the results are well documented - raised blood pressure, depression, lowered natural defenses and immune function, and so on. The effects of stress are even felt with changes that are seen as beneficial - a promotion at work, an upcoming wedding, or winning the lottery, although we more often relate stress to the difficulties and challenges that are part of our experience.

How much does stress have to do with the breakdown of our health and susceptibility to conditions such as cancer, and how much is genetics? An interesting study in The New England Journal of Medicine reported that when people had been adopted at birth, their cancer risk matched that of their adopted parents, rather than their biological parents. Dr. David Schreiber says that at most, genetic factors supply 15 percent to an individual's cancer risk. Obviously, there is much more than genetics involved in our overall health. How we handle stress and what lifestyle choices we make may account for much of that remaining 85 percent.

There are many well-known steps to good health - exercise and eating well among them. There are also many simple practices that can greatly contribute to strengthening our immune systems and natural defenses. We can't totally avoid stress, but we can learn to respond differently to our internal and external environments in order to lower harmful stress hormones. Incorporating a regular practice of yoga, tai chi, qigong, or meditation can reduce stress, strengthen the immune system, and teach us methods to restore our center of calmness and balance even in the midst of a difficult situation. Utilizing deep, slow breathing is another technique that can instantly transform the inner environment.

Regular physical activity such as walking or gardening has been shown to improve health and even increase survival rates for many types of cancer. As I (Cheryl) discovered in my research when I was diagnosed with advanced cancer many years ago, cancer doesn't grow in oxygen. Since the type of cancer I had tended to metastasize to the lungs, oxygenating my lungs through aerobic walking was a practical response. Exercise reduces stress hormones and when combined with nature, as in gardening or walking in a beautiful, natural setting, also increases the production of beneficial endorphins.

As important as it is to treat your body well - to give it good nutrition, exercise, sunshine, rest, and so on - it's even more important to think good thoughts. As Peace Pilgrim liked to say, negative thoughts affect you more quickly than eating junk foods. Your thoughts instantly create physical reactions. Just think about a time when you've woken up from a scary dream with heart pounding and pulse racing. Although dreams take place in the imagination of your subconscious mind, your body responds physically.

Thoughts have an affect on all of the functions of the body and repeated negative thoughts can trigger changes that lead to physical difficulties. Type A personalities, for example, people whose tendencies are toward an excessive competitive drive and who exhibit easily aroused hostilities, have been linked to cardiovascular disorders. Cancer has sometimes been linked to lost relationships, a difficulty in expressing anger, or feelings of unworthiness or self-dislike. Constant worry or long term stress has been linked to ulcers. Although science may not consider worry to be a cause of ulcers, it recognizes stress as sometimes playing a contributing role.

The habitual tone of our thoughts affects a physical response. If this is so, what is the state of your own thinking? Thoughts that empower, uplift, inspire, give hope, tune you into your positive potential, are healing thoughts. They sew the seeds of good health.

Thoughts that disempower you, bring you down, are critical of yourself or others, make you feel guilty or unworthy, are dis-ease producing thoughts.

The first step toward sowing empowering thoughts is to pay attention to your thinking and thought patterns. Are there areas in your thinking that are motivated by underlying negative beliefs? This job is such a pain in the neck, such organ language as an ongoing thought mantra, is a pretty obvious precursor to creating some problem, whether job frustration or stress leading to physical dis-ease (like a chronic stiff neck). When you catch yourself in a negative frame of mind, change your thinking. There is always a positive side. The experience I'm gaining in this job is going to help me get the job of my dreams.

Once you've gotten those thoughts in order, turn your attention to your body. If you had only one suit of clothes or outfit to wear, you'd take very good care of it. This body is it - your one suit of clothes. There is no exchanging it, so it makes sense to take good care of it. And let's not forget the mind-body connection. Just as your thoughts affect your body, your body affects your thoughts. Clog up the body with high fat and cholesterol, don't exercise or get enough sleep, never mind about sunshine and fresh air, and what happens to the mind? It forgets what it feels like to be sharp, to be in control, to have those creative ideas flow. The body nourishes the mind, the mind nourishes the body, and spirit nourishes both.

The general climate of your emotions is another important area to explore. Stuck emotions have been called a root of illness. An interesting study on cancer therapy came from Germany. Dr. Ryke-Geerd Hamer, a medical doctor and cancer surgeon, examined more than 20,000 patients with all types of cancer, over a period of 10 years. Hamer observed that in all of his patients, cancer did not spread directly from one organ to the surrounding tissue. For example, he noted that if a patient had cancer of the cervix it never spread to the uterus.

His interviews also began to show that before the onset of illness, every one of his patients had experienced some kind of emotional or psychic conflict that had not been satisfactorily resolved. As Hamer compiled records of these patients he also took X-rays of their brains. In each case the X-rays showed a "dark shadow" in some particular area that corresponded to a specific type of cancer. According to Hanne Born, "There was also a 100% correlation between the dark spot in the brain, the location of the cancer and the specific type of unresolved conflict."

The result of this research has led Hamer to conclude that when a person suffers from a stressful conflict that is not resolved, the particular emotion being felt (anger, frustration, grief, fear and so on) lodges in an emotional response center in the brain that is connected to a specific organ. Over time that particular emotion center begins to break down and send faulty information to the organ that it controls, resulting in deformed or cancerous cells.

Hamer has also suggested that metastases, rather than indicating that cancer is spreading, is actually the result of new conflicts. These conflicts may even be the result of the very stress of having cancer and undergoing various invasive, painful or nauseating therapies.

With the inclusion of psychotherapy in treatment, Hamer found that as conflicts were resolved, cancer stopped growing at a cellular level. The dark shadow on the brain also began to disappear as diseased tissue was replaced by normal tissue. According to Hamer, research in Germany, Austria, France, the US and Denmark has confirmed his findings that there is an emotional component in the onset of cancer and that solving the conflicts in question stops the growth of cancer.

A healthy life is a life lived in balance and integrity. We can plant seeds of good health in all of the areas of our lives that make up the whole. The following guidelines, which can be expanded or contracted, are ways to move toward increased physical and psychological health, lower stress levels, and increased inspiration and enthusiasm for the gift that is your life:

1. A means of livelihood that is useful to society - something you enjoy doing. If you are retired or your livelihood is limited, give yourself fulfilling tasks such as support or encouragement to a neighbor or friend, volunteering, tending a garden, or "greening" your purchases or home cleaning products.

2. Include inspiration in your life - things that lift you up, such as special music or words or the beauty of nature. Fill your environment with inspiration.

3. Good living habits - regular exercise, sunshine, fresh air, food that nourishes the body, plenty of rest and good thoughts.

4. A path of service - something you do with an outgoing motive to be of service, without thought of receiving anything in return.

5. A quiet time each day spent practicing yoga, tai chi, qigong, meditation, non-goal oriented self-hypnosis or receptive silence.

No man lives unto himself; for every living thing is bound by cords to every other living thing. - The Aquarian Gospel

All things are connected like to blood that connects us all. Man did not weave the web of life, he is merely a strand in it. - Chief Seattle

No man is an island, entire of itself; every man is a piece of the continent, a part of the main. - John Donne

There is a loftier ambition than merely to stand high in the world. It is to stoop down and lift mankind a little higher. - Henry Van Dyke

We ourselves feel that what we are doing is but a drop in the ocean. But if that drop was not in the ocean, I think the ocean would be less because of that missing drop. - Mother Teresa

Into the hands of every individual is given a marvelous power for good or evil - the silent, unconscious, unseen influence of his life. This is simply the constant radiation of what man really is, not what he pretends to be. - William G. Gordan

Humanity can only improve as people improve. When you have improved your life, you can inspire those around you to want to improve their lives. Remember that a few in harmony with God's will are more powerful than multitudes out of harmony. – Peace Pilgrim

Our generation faces the greatest moral and political crisis in human history. Will we take the steps necessary to avert catastrophic global warming or will we doom our children to a new Dark Age in a world that is biologically and economically impoverished? Our grandchildren may look longingly at our era as the apex of civilization and human progress. - Robert F. Kennedy, Jr.

A human being is a part of the whole called by us universe, a part limited in time and space. He experiences himself, his thoughts and feeling as something separated from the rest, a kind of optical delusion of his consciousness. This delusion is a kind of prison for us, restricting us to our personal desires and to affection for a few persons nearest to us. Our task must be to free ourselves from this prison by widening our circle of compassion to embrace all living creatures and the whole of nature in its beauty. - Albert Einstein

CHAPTER 35

Our Part in the Whole

It is easy to see ourselves as individuals, separate from anything or anyone else - and from a limited perspective, there is truth in that. But it is a perspective that isolates one part from the whole, much like the difference between a drop of water that is separated from the ocean. Baird Spalding said, "The drop of water is only weak when it is removed from the ocean; replace it and it is as powerful as the ocean... If a portion of one unit excludes itself from the whole, it makes no difference to Principal Being, but it makes a vast difference to the unit. The ocean is not conscious of the removal of a drop of water, but the drop is very conscious of the ocean when it is returned."

Scientifically speaking, everything can be broken down into microscopic parts that reflect the macrocosm. You can actually go in either direction, focusing down to 37 trillion microscopic cells within your own body, each with consciousness and intelligence, to the macrocosm of the universe. Each is a system containing subsystems. You are conscious of your body being a whole unit, yet you are composed of subsystems that are not aware of the whole and function from a perception of being separate. Stretching this view in the other direction, you can also begin to recognize yourself as one cell in the body of humanity. Mahatma Gandhi put it in spiritual terms: "I believe that if one man gains spiritually the whole world gains with him and, if one falls, the whole world falls to that extent."

Much like a cancer cell that might experience itself as separate and perceive the rapid multiplying of itself as survival misses the big picture - that the act of reproducing out of harmony with the whole is ensuring its own demise, along with the unit of which it is part. We sometimes act in our human endeavors as though what we choose for ourselves does not affect the rest. This limited perspective lacks the bigger truth: that we are all connected, all one, all part of a larger totality. It is this view of the bigger picture that allows us to join in the universal flow of oneness and harmony that directs the universe. It is called by many names. Pierre Teilhard de Chardin called it love: "Love is the affinity which links and draws together the elements of the world... Love, in fact, is the agent of universal synthesis."

Looking back at the microcosm we see that each part of the body contributes some function that adds to the effectiveness of the whole body - the eyes do their job, the liver does its job, the heart, bones, blood, every cell, is programmed to perform its special roles. You can take this same view into your part in life. You have many roles. You are born male or female. You may marry or take on the role of a partner. If you choose to become a parent you enlarge the family unit. As an individual you have an affinity toward certain things, some of which you may take on as one of your roles. You may excel in sports or art or language or computer skills or mechanical ability or science or musical talent. You might tap into intellectual heights or compassionate heights or physical excellence or any number of things. Within all of those things that you love - the universal agent of synthesis - are your potential roles. Unfortunately, what often happens is that choices get made based on more superficial values like prestige or money or power.

An important factor in making choices regarding the roles we take on in life is the effect of our choices on the parts of which we are a whole. When we choose to be a partner, whether in a personal relationship or business, choices from that point on will affect each partner. When a business enlarges to include employees or a family of two enlarges to include children or elderly parents, choices now effect the entire group. This is the framework from which we begin to understand that we have a relationship with something bigger than ourselves. The development of this growing discernment ultimately leads us to the more expanded awareness of our part in the bigger whole – that of the human family.

What is our part, then, in the whole? On a very personal level, it is to develop and excel in those things that we love. It is then to direct those skills in ways that contribute a positive and harmonious influence around us and in the world. Here is where we are able to engage our passion and sense of direction.

On a collective level, it is hard not to see that we are living at a crisis period in human history. We are facing many critical choices, and all of us who are alive today play a part that will help to determine the direction of civilization. Are we going to allow whatever forces are in power take us on a path that leads toward destruction, annihilation or possibly extinction? Or will we be part of the stirring and awakening that needs to take place with sufficient movement to turn the tide? We are all helping to direct the outcome. When we do nothing, we are allowing the slide toward destruction to continue.

Martin Luther King, Jr. said, "Darkness cannot drive out darkness; only light can do that. Hate cannot drive out hate; only love can do that. Hate multiplies hate, violence multiplies violence, and toughness multiplies toughness in a descending spiral of destruction.... The chain reaction of evil - hate begetting hate, wars producing more wars - must be broken, or we shall be plunged into the abyss of annihilation."

We are all being called into action, and it is up to us to respond to the call. Lawrence Summers, President of Harvard University, says, "The only antidote to dangerous ideas is strong alternatives vigorously advocated." The survival of humankind and this planet is everyone's business. As we step into our part in the whole we can join forces, putting our strong and united efforts toward healing ourselves and our planet and tapping into the richness of our positive human potential.

The significant problems we face cannot be solved at the same level of thinking we were at when we created them. - Albert Einstein

The relationship between human civilization and the Earth has been utterly transformed by a combination of factors, including the population explosion, the technological revolution, and a willingness to ignore the future consequences of our present actions. – Al Gore

We live in one of the most interesting junctures in world history, a period that will shape the pathway for generations to come. There are two ways to approach these challenging times. We can hide our heads in the sand and hope for the best or proactively prepare and do our part to affect a positive outcome. - Todd Harrison

The laws of nature are just, but terrible. There is no weak mercy in them. Cause and consequence are inseparable and inevitable. – Henry W. Longfellow

No man can violate Nature's laws and escape her penalties. – Julian P. Johnson

It is difficult to get a man to understand something when his salary depends upon his not understanding it. – Upton Sinclair

Knowing the name of each wild thing is ultimately not very important. Such knowledge tells us little about the thing itself. That we would understand that each single creature is part of a complex tapestry enveloping the planet; That when a creature passes to extinction one more thread is removed from the design - when we understand that then we understand something about a wild animal more precious than its name. - Glendalough National Park Info Center

The dynamo of man's inventiveness has outstripped the dynamo of humanity again. To harmonize them is the only hope for our civilization. -Thomas A. Edison

The sun, the moon and the stars would have disappeared long ago... had they happened to be within the reach of predatory human hands. - Havelock Ellis

I think the environment should be put in the category of our national security. Defense of our resources is just as important as defense abroad. Otherwise what is there to defend? - Robert Redford

CHAPTER 36

Our Relationship to the Earth: The Great Challenge

Through birth we inherit a responsibility far beyond assuring our own survival. We must assure the survival and health of our planet for future generations. If we have been asleep to our spiritual foundation in this material world it is now time to arouse ourselves from this cultural trance and reclaim our heritage. We need to bring a more holistic awareness into focus so that we can use the tremendous insights and technological and scientific advancements we have attained to bring our lives and that of the earth back into balance. We are walking a knife's edge between the destruction wrought by violence and greed (which with modern technology could destroy our world) and the reconstruction and transformation that can only come through an awakening of our potential to be instruments of positive influence and change, working for the good of the whole.

In the words of Wayne Dyer, author of *You'll See It When You Believe It*, "Take a few moments to study the word 'universe,' the term that we use to describe this immense world of form in which we find ourselves thinking and breathing, day in and day out. Breaking the word down, we have 'uni,' meaning 'one,' and 'verse,' a 'song.' One song! That is our universe, my friends. Just one song. No matter how we separate into individual little notes, we are all still involved in the onesong."

We human beings are part of that universe, and part of the earth upon which we dwell. Too often, however, we experience ourselves as separate from the whole. We see ourselves as separate from our neighbors, separate from other tribes, separate from the rest of the world. This has created a limitation in our relationship to all but a few closest to us. For the sake of our health and survival - and that of the planet we inhabit - we need to broaden the circle of our compassion to embrace all life.

All of the parts of the earth and all of its inhabitants are interrelated. How then can we treat the earth, our physical environment, so poorly that we threaten our own existence? The very underpinning of our existence is breaking down as the building blocks of life on this planet are dying. The decline in phytoplankton, for example, the first photosynthesizing organism to appear, can be traced back to the destruction of our rain forests. As millions of acres of forests are cut down and burned (over one million in Brazil alone in one year) silt is being washed into deltas, killing off phytoplankton.

The burning and cutting of our forests is depleting oxygen in the lower atmosphere, where nearly all clouds and weather conditions occur, as well as the oceans. This decreasing oxygen is then unable to produce sufficient ozone in the stratosphere, the upper atmosphere. The resulting entry of ultraviolet rays causes more trees to die and the climate to change. The depleted ozone lets in more ultraviolet light, contributing to the rise of skin cancers and weakening immune systems in people. The decline of the earth's forests and ecosystems continues to escalate:

- For example, the years between 1970 and 1995, according to the World Wide Fund for Nature (WWF), the world's natural forest cover declined by .5 percent per year, for a total loss of 10 percent - the amount of forest lost equivalent to the size of England and Whales or half of Norway. These losses are continuing to this day.
- In the same 25-year period, WWF reported that a full third of the world's natural resources have been consumed.
- Freshwater ecosystems disappeared at a rate of six percent per year, halving in number in those 25 years.
- Marine ecosystems during that period dropped by 30 percent.
- In a 20-year period in our lifetimes, 64% of the ground cover in Africa was destroyed.

- Droughts are a legacy of ecological destruction. Richard Underwood, a retired NASA engineer has said, "There are large areas of Africa where it will never rain again."

We can't afford to believe that we can escape the consequences of short-term economic gains for corporate or self-interest. We can't afford to cover our eyes or to be deceived by lobby interests and corporate or personal greed. As concerned and responsible citizens, we must make sure that our elected representatives in Congress and parliaments throughout the world, regardless of party affiliation, are working for the good of the whole.

In many ways, collectively, we are living with a sense of separation from nature and the earth. It's much like living in a somnambulistic state in which we are not quite awake and not quite asleep. From this sleep-dream state we have allowed terrible destruction to occur. Since the 1990's over 97% of climate scientists have been in agreement that global warming is primarily man-made, as great a consensus as is found among scientists. Climate change is rewriting human civilization. It is already threatening to make parts of the world uninhabitable or highly inhospitable for the continuation of life as we know it. Global warming is contributing to an increase in poverty that will continue in a downward spiral, coastlines will be swamped and infrastructure destroyed.

A year after the major breakthrough of the Paris Climate Agreement, unanimously signed by 195 countries, the US announced its impending withdrawal in 2017, ignoring the most pressing global challenge civilization faces. There have been five mass extinctions before the one we're now causing that is getting underway. These extinctions, except for the one that killed the dinosaurs, were caused by climate change produced by greenhouse gas. As an incredible warning and wake up call today, we can look back to 252 million years ago, when an increase in seawater temperature of 10.8°F occurred. That warming caused the release of methane in the Arctic and decimated 97 percent of all life on earth. Today, carbon is being added to the atmosphere at a considerably faster and alarming rate, and accelerating.

The earth that will be left to our children (and our own future incarnations according to the beliefs of many) will be increasingly hotter, the air and waters will be dirtier, there will be more wildfires and more severe droughts, hurricanes and floods. We can only conjecture on what the effects of global warming will be on the earth and its inhabitants. The total ramifications are unknown.

The earth is the body that sustains us and all life on this planet, and it is being destroyed. We are living on the edge of unprecedented disaster. The alarm has been sounded over and over - as scientific fact. If we fail to heed that warning we are living in major denial or self-interested corruption. Species are disappearing. Ecosystems are collapsing. It is up to all of us who are alive at this time to stop the massacre. Albert Einstein left us this thought regarding the interrelatedness of life: "If the bee disappeared off the surface of the globe, then man would only have four years of life left. No more bees, no more pollination, no more plants, no more animals, no more man." A sobering reality: bee populations are declining rapidly for reasons that are as yet not fully determined, although the effects of pesticides are a major factor.

Most of the world's major environmental problems are continuing to accelerate exponentially. Our climate crisis is accelerating at a rate even beyond the previous dire warnings of climate scientists, in part as a result of feedback loops. For example, as permafrost of the Siberian tundra has begun to melt, tremendous amounts of methane (a greenhouse gas 20 times more potent than carbon dioxide) are now being released, thus further increasing global warming. Potentially even worse is the recent discovery of millions of tons of methane escaping into the atmosphere from beneath the Arctic seabed. Massive deposits of sub-sea methane are bubbling to the surface as the Arctic region becomes warmer and the ice retreats. Scientists believe that the sub-sea layer of permafrost has acted like a "lid" to prevent the gas from escaping, and giant positive feedback of higher temperatures could lead to further permafrost melting and the release of yet more of the enormous reserves of methane stored in the Arctic. There is now added concern that methane from the world's oceans could also begin to escape.

We must reclaim the value of life - all life - and our responsibility to leave a habitable, stable planet for countless generations to come. If individuals or conglomerates in power are jeopardizing our future they need to be stopped now, made accountable, and removed from positions of power and influence. The earth is not the domain of a handful of individuals. We all stand accountable for the consequences of our actions and our inactions in this critical time. When we join together, we increase our strength exponentially.

Most importantly, we can focus our life energy in positive, productive directions. Outrage may suffice to fire us up, but a steady output will drain us. If we get together and use all of the energy that we've spent condemning what has been or is being done, to promote and work toward the solutions we see fit, we will find ourselves moving much more effectively and speedily toward the goals we desire to see implemented. Let us imagine together what we can do. Let us pray together for vision and courage and direction. Let us take action as we work together to turn the tide of destruction toward the most positive outcome possible. It is too late to wait - but it is not too late to begin.

We are in an age of remarkable technological advances. Effectiveness and cost improvements in electronics, computers, the internet and the information superhighway are revolutionary. But if we don't make necessary important changes now, the continuing deterioration of our environment will be profoundly costly and solutions insufficient in the years ahead.

Our time of reckoning has come. Creating a sustainable planet isn't good enough, especially because of the destruction that has already occurred. We owe it to all future generations, and to ourselves, to go beyond just slowing or halting the destruction and begin restoring the Earth. Is it possible for us to turn things around and begin repairing rather than destroying our small planet? We still have the capacity to make great strides in this regard. And despite current jobs versus the environment rhetoric, the very doable solutions for ecological restoration will make the world healthier, safer, more prosperous and more secure for us and our children.

Against this somber backdrop and the urgency of a shrinking window of opportunity, there is also good news and reason for hope. We have leaders providing major insights and much needed bold solutions. Paul Hawken's *The Ecology of Commerce* was called "The most important book for the 21st Century." He then co-authored *Natural Capitalism* and in 2017 *Drawdown* was released. With thorough research backing a visionary new paradigm, all of these books describe transformative solutions to save business and our environment.

The Al Gore documentary *An Inconvenient Truth* was an Academy Award winner, and his climate crisis work also led to him being co-recipient of the 2007 Nobel Peace Prize. In 2017, *An Inconvenient Sequel: Truth to Power* was released. In *Our Choice: A Plan to Solve the Climate Crisis*, Gore writes that we have "all of the tools we need to solve the climate crisis. The only missing ingredient is collective will."

Lester Brown continues to offer major solutions in his book, *Plan B 4.0: Mobilizing to Save Civilization*. Like Hawken, Brown eloquently explains the crucial need of tax shifting, lowering income taxes while raising levies on environmentally destructive activities, which has become widely endorsed by economists.

Enron was the seventh most valuable corporation in the U.S. in early 2001. Then it was discovered that the company had been leaving certain costs off the books. With those costs, Enron was worthless. It quickly went bankrupt and no longer exists. Lester Brown points out that we are doing exactly what Enron did, leaving costs off the books, but on a far larger scale. If we persist in leaving out indirect costs that the market omits, he says "we will face the same fate as Enron."

Oystein Dahl, a former Vice President of Exxon, observed, "Socialism collapsed because it did not allow the market to tell the economic truth. Capitalism may collapse because it does not allow the market to tell the ecological truth."

The choices we make now will affect life on earth for all generations to come. Besides the major economic and legal changes that are needed, what we can do individually is crucial for the restoration of our planet and our future. Here are some examples:

- Vote with our dollars. Spend our money to support those products and services that support the sustainability of our earth and future generations.
- Eat low on the food chain.
- Buy organic food when possible.
- Buy from local farmers and farmer's markets.

- Build green; remodel with green features.
- If you need to use a car, choose a model that gets superior gas mileage and low emissions. If you can, get an electric car or hybrid. Walk, bike, car pool, or take public transportation when possible.
- Recycle all potentially recyclable materials.
- Activate the democratic process. Vote responsibly.

Things we can do collectively:

- Work for solutions. Support sustainable alternatives (like harvesting pharmaceutical herbs from rainforests rather than destroying ecosystems).
- Support the development of technologies which could eliminate dependence on fossil and nuclear fuel.
- Begin to re-grow forests from the edges out to restore a normal, healthy cloud building process to the planet.
- Attend community meetings.

We have a moral directive to move toward positive changes that will affect all aspects of life for the better. Inaction at this time will allow forces causing permanent destruction to continue accelerating toward increasingly unmanageable levels. To continue with destructive leaning is to leave the overwhelming legacy of even greater toxic waste, resource depletion, over-population, rising oceans and out-of-control accelerating global warming to the next generation. With the rapid industrialization in many developing countries and billions yearning for the cars and conveniences of industrialized societies, the ecological mathematics don't even begin to work out without revolutionary transformation.

There is great divisiveness in the world today. That divide has to do with power, economics, politics, self versus greater good, ignorance, and the repercussions of short-sighted choices being made that will affect all of us. The earth hangs in the balance as do future generations. We are all being called to wake up, take action, support the greater good and do our part. Millions of us need to reach inside to find our individual role in the awakening and unfolding that will lead us to an envisioned Golden Age of inner and outer transformation.

The following are some of the resources that offer important solutions.

Books:

Paul Hawken, *The Ecology of Commerce*, Revised Edition

Hawken, Lovins & Lovins, *Natural Capitalism: Creating the Next Industrial Revolution.*

Paul Hawken, *Drawdown*: The Most Comprehensive Plan Ever Proposed to Reverse Glabal Warming

Lester Brown, *Plan B 4.0: Mobilizing to Save Civilization*

Al Gore, *Our Choice: A Plan to Solve the Climate Crisis*

Worldwatch Institute, EarthEd (State of the World): *Rethinking Education on a Changing Planet*

Peter Brannen, *The Ends of the World*

David Wallace-Wells, *The Uninhabitable Earth*

Joseph Romm, *Climate Change: What Everyone Needs to Know*

Websites:

Union of Concerned Scientists: www.ucsusa.org

350.org: www.350.org

The Climate Reality Project: www.climaterealityproject.org

Worldwatch Institute: www.worldwatch.org

Environmental Defense Fund: www.edf.org

National Resources Defense Council (NRDC): www.nrdc.org

World Wide Fund for Nature (WWF): www.worldwildlife.org

Al Gore: www.algore.com

Adam Trombly, Institute for Advanced Studies at Aspen: www.Project Earth.com

Documentaries:

An Inconvenient Truth

An Inconvenient Sequel: Truth to Power

The souls of people, on their way to Earth-life, pass through a room full of lights; each takes a taper - often only a spark - to guide it in the dim country of this world. But some souls, by rare fortune, are detained longer - have time to grasp a handful of tapers, which they weave into a torch. These are the torch-bearers of humanity - its poets, seers and saints, who lead and lift the race out of darkness, toward the light. They are the law-givers and saviors, the light-bringers, way-showers and truth-tellers, and without them, humanity would lose its way in the dark. - Plato

In the days ahead we must not consider it unpatriotic to raise certain basic questions about our national character. We must begin to ask, why are there 40 million poor people in a nation overflowing with such unbelievable affluence? Why has our nation placed itself in the position of being God's military agent on earth...? Why have we substituted the arrogant understanding of policing the whole world for the high task of putting our own house in order? - Martin Luther King, Jr.

Everyone here has the sense that right now is one of those moments when we are influencing the future. - Steve Jobs

Ideals are like stars; you will not succeed in touching them with your hands. But like the seafaring man on the desert of waters, you choose them as your guides, and following them you will reach your destiny. - Carl Schultz

If we are to change our world view, images have to change. The artist now has a very important job to do. He's not a little peripheral figure entertaining rich people, he's really needed. - Vaclav Havel

Non-violence leads to the highest ethics, which is the goal of all evolution. Until we stop harming all other living beings, we are still savages. - Thomas Edison

Beyond the beliefs of any religion there is the truth of the human spirit. Beyond the power of nations, there is the power of the human heart. Beyond the ordinary mind, the power of wisdom and love and healing energy are at work in the universe. When we can find peace within our hearts, we contact these universal powers. This is our only hope. - Tharthang Tulku

CHAPTER 37

Ushering in a Golden Age

We think of a Golden Age as a time when peace and abundance will be the condition of the world. At a time of rampant war and violence it feels very far away. Will we ever reach a period when a Golden Age will be a reality? We can be sure that it won't come on its own. Peace will not come as long as our choices are based on fear or greed or arrogance. Peace will not come through hatred and distrust. Peace will not come through breaking Universal Laws of compassion and non-violence. It will only come when enough of us are ready to pay the price of peace.

What is the price of peace? The price of peace is to turn from fear to faith in the living of higher laws. We need to give more than lip service to spiritual values. We need to live the spiritual laws that we profess to believe in. It takes faith to act from the courage of our convictions. There is never a time when Universal Law (or whatever name we give to that underlying governing force) advocates or condones acts of violence, hatred or greed. We must look to the guidance of true spiritual leaders, untouched by the musings and rationalizations of political or private agendas.

There is no "us against them" although many of us like to believe that is so. They are us and we are them. We come from the same source and we are made from the same stuff. There is only one earth and we share it with all other countries and cultures. War and violence make as much sense as solving a dispute with our neighbor by teaching our sons and daughters how to use weapons and sending them across the street to do our killing for us. Never mind if young children or innocent people get in the way. That's just the sacrifice it takes to assert our will.

We can't see the blood, we can't feel the pain or devastation, until it is "us" that gets hit. Until it is our children, our husbands and wives, that don't return or only partially come back, or until in retaliation and hatred it is our country, our buildings, our civilians. We will not be free from such terror until we are willing to stand before the world tribunal with clean hands and moral integrity. Until we are willing to sanction and stand behind strong, peaceful negotiations for the good of all people in all countries.

As Ghandi pointed out, an eye for an eye will make the whole world blind. We will never overcome violence with more violence. That will only increase the violence. It is time to search our national conscience: Who are the evildoers? As long as we sanction war, we are sanctioning the training of our youth in methods of mass killing and destruction. We are sending them off prepared to kill someone else's parent, partner, child - or to be killed or maimed. We are sacrificing their lives and limbs, their innocence and morality, their very souls. We collectively carry the blood on our hands no matter how far away or objective it might seem. "Just press the lever here. There goes the bomb. Right on target!" And now there are unmanned aerial vehicles, known as drones - controlled by 'pilots' on the ground or following a pre-programmed mission. Not combat in this case, but targeted killing. Drone killing in America would certainly be met with disbelief, outrage and condemnation.

The contest that we are witnessing in the world today is between the war way of attempting to overcome evil with evil, which with modern weapons can lead to complete chaos, and the peace way of overcoming evil with good. This way could lead to the ushering in of a truly Golden Age. If we want peace, we need to live the peace we want to see in the world. On a national level. On an individual level. On a personal level. On a heart and soul level.

The world may seem wildly out of control but we are not helpless. We have control over ourselves. We can find meaning and purpose in life by living with meaning and purpose. We are the architects of our own inner world, and we help to construct the world around us – with our thoughts, with our words, and with our actions. The outer world is a reflection of the collective inner situation. We can see the immaturity, the greed, the self-serving. Yet beneath that there is also incredible potential for good. If we look for the good we can find it. We can appeal to that good. We can call it out of the shadows where the hero in all of us is waiting to be discovered.

The Golden Age is symbolic of a time when we have collectively learned the ways of peace. But we don't have to wait for the outer manifestation of that vision. Each of us is capable of making a choice to usher in the Golden Age now – inside of ourselves. We start by putting into practice the highest principles we know. By living with compassion and good intention. As former Congressman Dennis Kucinich put it, "The world is multidimensional. The new vision is a holistic one that understands the power of intention and the power of cooperation, of mutuality, of trust, of seeing the world as one. That vision then becomes our outer reality. Ours is the ability, through our consciousness, to create peace, to create love. The organ of transformation is the human heart because there is nothing - no weapon ever made - that is more powerful than a human heart."

Outer change will come when enough individuals make the choice every day to model maturity and compassion; to use our resources wisely to protect the earth that supports us; to refuse to make choices that compromise our integrity or hold the rights of any group or nation superior over any other; and to vote for elected officials who reflect these same higher values and who are willing to work without self-centered interests for the good of the whole.

Inner change will come as soon as we make these choices for ourselves; as soon as we set forth our intention to live up to the highest beliefs we hold and act on those intentions, practicing them until we have perfected them. Inner change will come when we consciously reach for the good in people and in ourselves. As we change and heal ourselves, we are helping to lay the foundation for a new renaissance. We are becoming a part of the spiritual awakening and stirring that will lead to a Golden Age. Whenever, however it comes, we will be prepared because we ourselves will have found it inside.

Regression Hypnotherapy, 2nd Edition
Transcripts of Transformation, Volume I

The "Ultimate Teaching Text" by Randal Churchill

An intimate view of profound therapy by America's leading regression teacher.
Winner of the Founders Award for Excellence in Professional Literature

New release! Announcing the updated and expanded 2nd Edition of this classic text. Randal Churchill has taught his pioneering regression work to thousands of therapists for four decades. In this fascinating, well-organized and responsible training guide, he uses his unique style to weave together a **powerful combination of methods to heal underlying issues for deeply transforming therapy.**

There has been **a strong need for more comprehensive literature in the extremely important field of regression therapy.** Guidance and details regarding therapeutic options is severely limited in most books. Almost all books on the topic provide little or no information on various powerful and crucial forms of the work, such as the integration of Gestalt, and protective and exploratory ideomotor methods.

Regression Hypnotherapy gives the reader an inside look at the **tremendous range of possibilities** available for regression strategies. With great skill and sensitivity, the author integrates a wealth of effective options, utilizing **15 Major Steps in Emotional Clearing Regression**. Comprehensive strategies often include regressing to initial sensitizing events, emotional clearing, uncovering misconceptions and doing reeducation. Riveting transcripts and commentary complement chapters providing clearly written principles, documenting the profound potential of this work.

"*Regression Hypnotherapy*, by Randal Churchill, is destined to become **an instant classic and will be used by hypnotherapists for decades to come. This ultimate teaching text** is highly recommended for all in the field."

-Ormond McGill, *The Dean of American Hypnotists*
Author of over 25 books

432 pages, hardbound, with a beautiful dust cover. Printed on acid-free, natural recycled paper with soy-based ink.

Visit **www.transformingpress.com**, for more information, including the Table of Contents, Preface, reviews, a sample chapter, special **savings**, & an order form for an autographed copy.

Email Transforming Press at: TransformP@aol.com

Here are Comments from HTI Graduates

please see the ad on the next page

"You certainly covered a broad range of modalities, but I was most impressed by your depth, especially during the therapy demonstrations. You are both **masters of reaching the underlying issues and working through profoundly challenging problems.** You are so skillful, sensitive and supportive, I would send anyone in the world to you."

-Dr. Victoria West, Chiropractor, Fremont, CA

"...I returned to North Carolina with **the tools and the confidence to build a successful practice in an area where other hypnotherapists told me it couldn't be done.** Randal and the other instructors put heart and soul into every lesson and every demonstration. The seeds they planted three years ago continue to grow within me to this day. **My practice is thriving, and practicing hypnotherapy is the most fulfilling work I've ever done**. Attending HTI was the **best investment of time and money I've ever made."**

-Priscilla Broussard, CHt, Swannanoa, NC

"In my blind assumption that this was merely a fine school for the training of hypnotherapists, I found myself walking willingly into a safe and loving cocoon. In this place, I experienced and witnessed spiritual transformation and personal growth unparalleled in any other single event of my life. **The depth and breadth of the wisdom and knowledge offered to your students far exceeded my wildest expectations**, and the deep bonding I accomplished with the class I will carry in my heart forever."

-Catherine Hershon, CHt, Marketing Researcher, Scottsdale, AZ

"It's very hard to find the words to express my profound gratitude and appreciation for everything I was privileged to witness in class - **it was almost like a fairy-tale where miracles can be worked easily, effortlessly, and joyfully.** Everything was performed with great skill, experience, feeling, respect, and deep love."

-Tanya Konyukhova, CHt, Translator, Moscow, Russia

"The moment I arrived, I knew this was it. This is what I've been searching for for over three decades. I was literally **bursting with excitement, experiencing new worlds with each new lesson**.... In the years that I've been working as a hypnotherapist I've met many others in the same field. What arrests my attention is that although some of these people have attended excellent schools they have not the broad range of knowledge that I have acquired at HTI..."

-Mary Caldwell, CHt, Charlotte, NC

"I have taken **many hundreds of hours of training** in hypnotherapy from a wide variety of training programs in the US and abroad. From first-hand experience, the training program offered at HTI with Randal Churchill and Cheryl Canfield is the **best hypnotherapy training program available today**...."

-Kenneth A. Kern, MD, MPH, San Diego, CA